DONE WITH DATING

Done
WITH
Dating

7 Steps
to Finding
Your Person

Samantha Burns, MA, LMHC

**ROCKRIDGE
PRESS**

Interior and Cover Designer: Rachel Haeseker
Photo Art Director/Art Manager: Sue Bischofberger
Editor: Pippa White
Production Editor: Ashley Polikoff
Photography: © Christi Tolbert/shutterstock

Author photo courtesy of Susan Walker/Elia Photography

ISBN: Print 978-1-64152-540-4| eBook 978-1-64152-541-1

To D.G.S. and T.R.S., the loves of my life

CONTENTS

INTRODUCTION

You're sick of being single. You're wondering why all of your friends have found their mates and you're still alone. Maybe you're tired of the pressure your family is putting on you to settle down. You feel like it shouldn't be this hard. Maybe you've recently gone through a breakup or a divorce and are nervous about getting back out there. You don't want to settle for an unsatisfying relationship, and you doubt whether you can find that physical chemistry *and* someone who feels like your best friend. If you have to swipe left one more time you're going to scream! You think you're fabulous, so why do you keep attracting dating duds and one-and-dones? You've got your career or educational path all figured out but can't seem to get it together in your love life. Or, maybe all aspects of your life feel out of control, and you don't know where to start, but you know you need to get your act together. Perhaps you're struggling with low self-esteem and wondering if you're always going to have to settle. You're starting to question what's wrong with you. *Am I unlovable? Am I doomed to be alone forever?* The answer to those questions is no.

As a licensed counselor and coach specializing in dating, breakups, and relationships, I've committed my life to helping women address these questions and create the love lives they want and deserve. I don't just approach it from a clinical perspective, but a personal one because, girl, I've been there, too. I've had my fair share of dating war stories, struggling to get the commitment or quality of guy I desired. I hit rock bottom after a soul-crushing breakup with the man I thought I was going to marry, which ultimately led to my biggest personal growth, inspiring me to lift myself out of the trenches and employ a more strategic approach to dating. After creating an enjoyable dating life with a jam-packed dating schedule, I wound up meeting my husband a few months (and intense emotional journey) after my big breakup. I've been happily married to my best friend for more than five years now. So between my own experiences and the hundreds of women I've helped, I want you to rest assured, you're in good hands!

This book is for anyone who identifies as a woman and is looking for a genuine romantic connection, whether you're 18 or 75. Most dating books take a heteronormative approach, but this one is all-inclusive, since everyone is looking for love, not just straight cis women. That said, men can benefit from my advice, too, and any combination LGBTQ individuals seeking whomever they're attracted to. Love is love. By opening this book, you are allowing me to be your dating guru, your self-esteem cheerleader, your confidence coach. I'm here to guide you toward your last first date. You deserve someone who will love you fiercely and put in the same effort that you do to create a committed, secure, intimate relationship with open communication, trust, and affection. But don't kick back and relax too much—this book requires you to do more than simply read if you want to see true transformation in your dating life. You must take inspired action. If you're taking the time to read this, then make the time to implement the suggested changes. Love yourself enough to do the work.

This isn't one of those books that tells you what *not* to do, or gives you restrictive, outdated, sexist rules. Rather than gimmicks and prescribed formulas that give you one-size-fits-all dating rules by telling you that you have to look or act a certain way, this book is all about empowering you to feel comfortable and confident being *you*. That's because authenticity and vulnerability are the sexiest traits you have, and once you learn to embrace both of them, you will attract the love of your life. So let's debunk the myth once and for all that you have to be someone other than yourself to receive love. Honor your worth, respect your body, and recognize your inherent value. Are there some tweaks you can make to improve your love life to meet the type of people you're hoping to attract? Definitely. My suggestions are in this book, but at the end of the day, please know you are enough just as you are.

Now is your chance to get educated and take responsibility for creating the relationship you've always desired. Many of us had poor role models, unrealistic expectations, or were hurt along the way, and as a result, we learned to put up with less than we deserve. I truly believe that everyone deserves epic love. You deserve this love from yourself and from a partner. This book is unique because it begins with a focus on *you*. Once you learn to love yourself and accept your imperfections, you'll attract someone who loves and accepts you, too. So, before we begin, let's give up the idea of being perfect or of finding a perfect person—neither of those things exist. However, there is a perfectly imperfect partner out there for you. In fact, there are many people out there who could make fabulous partners, not just "The One" that you have to find out of millions of people on earth. That's because you don't find a soul mate, you create one. In this book I'll lay the foundation for how to choose a partner with long-term potential that's specific to your needs and desires, but then it's up to you to invest ongoing effort to nurture the relationship and grow together in the long run.

By banishing harmful shame stories and throwing out narratives that keep you playing small, you'll shift your mind-set and prioritize self-love. This will fill your life with joy and allow you to practice new dating approaches that were out of reach before. You'll finally be on your way to living your best life and going on your last first date!

Step

1

CHOOSE
WHO YOU ARE

YOUR DATING PROCESS doesn't begin when you show up on a first date, or when you send a first message, or even when you identify a list of what you desire in a partner. It starts when you carve out the time to become an expert on yourself. You can't get clear on who your ideal match is until you get clear on who you are. This will set the foundation for becoming a smarter, more intentional dater. Though you may feel confident that you already know yourself and be tempted to skip ahead to the juicy dating strategies, I urge you to take the time in this step to open your mind and thoughtfully meet yourself so that you can fall in love with *you* first.

SET A FOUNDATION WITHIN YOURSELF

Before building a structure, you must clear out anything that's in the way. This is true of constructing a house, and it's true of constructing your love life. If you want a healthy love life, follow me on this journey as we start with the root causes of modern-day dating problems.

Let's begin with a little context and real talk. As women in modern-day America, we are influenced by a host of unseen forces that affect the way we think about ourselves and the way we act. The long-standing patriarchal society we live in has conditioned women to play small (literally—to take up less space) and to be submissive (to be quieter, to wait to be told what to do, etc.). Whether or not you can see evidence of this in your own life, we have internalized that it's bad to be assertive, to be "bossy," to ask for what we want, and to set boundaries. And this has negatively impacted our self-esteem and created strife in our dating lives across the board.

Beyond those societal factors are the facts of our individual upbringings. Your levels of self-worth and self-acceptance are conditioned in early childhood. From infancy, your caregivers' behaviors taught you whether to believe that people are dependable or unreliable, whether people are attentive or inattentive, and whether love is given unconditionally or only under certain conditions. Growing up with neglectful or abusive parents, friends who betray you, and partners who cheat or lie can imbue you with the idea that you're not deserving of more before you're old enough to truly process these experiences.

Peer relationships in childhood and adolescence also influenced whether you felt accepted or whether you felt like the odd one out. (Female friendships in particular can be very challenging and often involve cruel bullying.) Your first crush and romantic interests impacted whether you felt attractive and desired, or rejected and not good enough.

All of these relational experiences affected the relationship you have with yourself today, including your level of self-respect and value, and ultimately whether you feel worthy of love from a partner. If no one has given you a reason to think you're incredible, it's pretty hard to believe you are. I'm here to tell you that a fulfilling, honest, and magnificent love is out there for you even if life has taught you otherwise.

If none of this resonates personally—if you feel that you had a safe, secure upbringing, and you received support and love, or you feel that your self-esteem is intact, but you're still struggling to date—stick with this step. I bet something here will click for you that you never realized before. At the end of the day, we are humans—and as such, we are sensitive creatures. It doesn't take a major childhood trauma to affect our sense of self or the way we act with others.

Ultimately the challenge with falling in love with yourself is that self-love is not formed in a solitary bubble—our interpersonal relationships impact it tremendously, whether we realize it or not. How do you tolerate being treated? Do you surround yourself with people who lift you up and bring out the best in you, or those who are takers, manipulative, or emotionally unavailable? Barriers to self-love include constantly comparing yourself to others, allowing others' standards to dictate the way you live your life instead of choosing and accepting your own ideals, and buying into the mind-set that you have to change yourself in order to receive love.

Confront the Past

This is your opportunity to redefine yourself and your standards. Once you do, love will have a path to follow.

Strengthen your sense of self by exploring your emotional needs, identifying your triggers, and taking an honest look at how you've been hurt so that you can avoid repeating negative patterns that you developed as coping mechanisms for that hurt. By exploring your past with open eyes and self-compassion, you can create your future with intention. Only then can you fill your life with things and people that bring you joy.

There's a chance you've been telling yourself the same narrative your entire life. Since you were young, you may have attributed the poor way other people treated you to some perceived internal flaws and negative traits. *I must be too needy, sensitive, annoying, lazy, stupid, boring, insecure, nerdy, introverted, loud, quiet, short, tall, fat, awkward, ugly.* Or, in contrast, your defense mechanism may be labeling problems with everyone else and taking no accountability for your behaviors. We love to label and categorize ourselves; this could look like giving yourself permission to constantly run late because you call yourself a procrastinator, believing your nose is too big for your face so you shy away from the camera, or perpetually being on a diet because someone called you chunky as a kid. Our labels tend to stick with us throughout our lives unless we really reflect on them and take action to shake them. We allow these internalized messages to create limiting beliefs about what we can accomplish, who we can be, and what we deserve. We allow them to dominate our life choices. Whether you've noticed it or not, you use these as excuses for why you're still single, why you settled for less than you deserved in the past, and why you tolerated unhealthy or nonreciprocal relationships.

Over the years in my practice, one of the biggest mistakes I've seen people make is that they treat their thoughts as facts, when they are actually only ideas or stories you've made up in your head. Think about this for a minute. Your thoughts are not facts. Your automatic thoughts impact your mood, then your behaviors, and eventually create your reality. What kind of reality are you living in? Is it kind or punishing? For instance, when looking in the mirror you might think, "I look gross and hate the way my stomach hangs over my jeans," which makes you feel sad or disgusted, and could lead to a number of dysfunctional behaviors, such as restricting food, binge eating your feelings, or not dating because you don't want anyone to see your body. Eventually these feelings and behaviors create an exaggerated and negative self-concept. You believe you're unhappy because you're fat and doomed to be alone forever because, well, how could anyone love you with that body? Okay, I know that sounds extreme—maybe that's not you exactly—but hopefully you can see how easily one can get sucked down the rabbit hole into a dark place just by engaging in a single destructive thought.

When you engage in negative thoughts about yourself, you're creating a reality in which you don't love yourself. On a daily basis, how are you perpetuating your insecurities and fears? Are you engaging in thoughts that no longer serve you? What if you took all the time that you typically beat yourself up and replaced it with only positive, affirming thoughts? For example, "I love the way I look in these jeans!" or, if that's a total stretch, at least give yourself a compliment rather than focusing on what you don't like. It's a conscious choice to refuse to criticize and only compliment yourself. Imagine how happy you could be, and the mental relief you'd feel from finally accepting yourself as enough, without having to change anything about yourself other than your thoughts. If you're instantly resistant to this idea, start by replacing any criticisms with simply more realistic thoughts. It's not that you're deluding yourself into believing you don't have a muffin top in those jeans; you're just choosing an alternative thought rather than berating yourself. Maybe the solution is to pick a different pair of pants that are more flattering, without standing in the mirror criticizing yourself for twenty minutes first. You don't need to live in a fantasy world, just a kinder one.

The way to change your old narrative is to flip the script and challenge the stinkin' thinkin' that's bringing you down. The good news is that you can write a new narrative. It starts with replacing your head trash with more realistic or positive thoughts, then taking small daily actions to support this new mentality. You can't change the past, but you can recognize where your emotional injuries come from, and then make a choice to stop defining yourself by old hurts, rejections, and beliefs. Only then can you take a fresh look at yourself—all of your unique qualities and quirks that make you different from anyone else in the entire world, your irresistible traits and personality, and the wonderful gifts that you can offer a lucky future partner just by being you. Right now, commit to investigating your emotional wounds without any preconceived notions of what you will find. It's possible to make a mental, physical, emotional, and spiritual transformation, but only if you are truly invested in being honest with yourself.

For the next section, I encourage you to get a notebook and physically write out your answers to each prompt or question. It sounds silly, but sometimes you don't even realize you're having a certain thought or reaction until you see it written down in your own words. And handwriting is more effective than typing in this regard; research shows that it helps convey emotions and intimate feelings, so I encourage you to actually handwrite your answers. If you prefer, though, you can type them out on your phone or computer. The important thing is to force yourself to answer each question in your own words rather than simply thinking your answers.

Try the following exercise so that you can say goodbye to your old narrative.

1. Write down your biggest pain points or shame stories. These are defining moments in your life that made you feel unworthy of love, not good enough, rejected, controlled, or hurt. Briefly account what happened, how it made you feel, and what harmful beliefs you internalized because of each experience. Once you've written your story down, ask yourself the following questions:

   * If you had to summarize your internalized belief into one sentence or statement about yourself, what would it be?

   * What patterns or behaviors did you develop to protect yourself from this shame and hurt?

   * Recognizing that your defenses no longer serve you and may be preventing you from true connection, what actions can you take to be more vulnerable?

   Here's an example from my life: In high school, I found out that my boyfriend of three years (which felt like forever at that age) had been unfaithful throughout our relationship. When I confronted him about my infidelity suspicions, he made me feel crazy, jealous, and insecure, which prevented me from being able to trust my gut and own judgment. (This is called gaslighting, by the way.) His gaslighting caused me to be clingy and fearful, and to ditch time with my friends so that I could keep my eye on him, which ended up alienating me from my friends as well. Because of this, I felt not only rejected by him, but also abandoned by my girlfriends, who were hurt and annoyed with my behavior. I felt completely alone, and as though no matter how much love I poured into the relationship, it was never enough to make him treat me the way I wanted him to, so I internalized the story that I was just *not enough*. This narrative then followed me into completely different relationships with different people. In fact, I carried the story around with me unknowingly until I finally looked it square in the face and realized that it was just a story I'd made up to try to make sense of what I was going through at the time.

2. Once you've spent some time with your story, and you feel comfortable, share your story or stories with a trusted companion, whether it's a best friend, therapist, or coach, since it's important to not let these stories perpetuate your shame in silence. Shame is healed in love. Allow an empathetic ear to bear witness to your pain and shame, and help you see that you matter.

3. Once you've shared your experiences, alone or with your support person, use a separate piece of paper to write down the main takeaways that you told yourself that aren't true and that you want to let go of. Go to a place where it's safe to burn things, and light that paper on fire to symbolically free yourself from the baggage that's keeping you stuck in your old narrative. As you watch the paper go up in flames, thank each experience and story because after all, they helped shape you into who you are today—a resilient, strong woman who is committed to learning about herself, evolving, and creating an epic love story.

4. Write down your three biggest criticisms or complaints about yourself. (These have likely stemmed from stories you have been carrying around.) Then, cross each one out and replace it with a more neutral or positive statement. For example, "I don't think I'm beautiful" can become "I feel the most beautiful when I . . ." (e.g., "am laughing," "get a blow out," "put on my favorite dress," "tell a good joke").

Treat Yourself the Way You Want to Be Treated

Now comes the fun part: You get to practice self-love. Self-love isn't an end state that once achieved will forever remain. It's more helpful to think of it as an ongoing practice, where it's cultivated and nurtured on a day-by-day basis. Practicing self-love allows you to get into the habit of treating yourself the way you deserve to be treated. This is important because by treating yourself the way you want someone else to treat you, you will develop the muscle for recognizing what good treatment feels like. It will help you restore your internal barometer for what a good and bad romantic relationship feels like.

When you hear the expression "love yourself first," what this really means is that you have to authentically meet yourself first. It's hard to love yourself if you don't know yourself. Sure, you can love someone else before you love yourself, but the problem is that the type of love you're willing to receive in return will reflect the low standards you have for yourself.

Self-love occurs when you honor yourself, define your own worth, assert your opinions, and operate from the mind-set that you're enough without having to change who you are. You don't have to love every ounce of yourself in order to respect yourself and live a meaningful life. We all have imperfections, and cultivating self-love is about the balance of accepting yourself as is, while also still giving yourself permission to grow and be your best self. It starts with looking for value inside of yourself, instead of letting others dictate what's cool or preferable. It's knowing inherently that you are worthy of love and are a catch. It's *not* about thinking that you're only good or attractive enough if you can get someone else to like you and want to date you. Commit to one of the following acts of self-love every day:

»→ Treat your body well; it's the only one you get. Fuel it with healthy food, exercise, and move in ways that give you strength and confidence.

»→ Give yourself ample time to recharge your mental batteries, especially when you're stressed and sleep-deprived.

»→ Set boundaries; hold yourself back from people-pleasing and focus on your own needs. Evaluate the people in your life. After spending time with each person, do you feel uplifted and happy? Or depleted and sad? Examine it and consider spending less time with anyone who is not adding to your life. Be honest with yourself about who might need to be removed permanently. The goal is to surround yourself with only people who support you.

»→ Create a gratitude practice where you identify one thing every day that you appreciate or are thankful for in your life.

»→ Embrace your intuition, and trust your gut when making decisions.

»→ Every time you glance in the mirror, give yourself one genuine compliment about your appearance, accomplishments, or personality traits. Whenever you notice that you're criticizing yourself or calling yourself a name, apologize and make one positive affirmation that's kind and compassionate.

»→ Do your best to be mindful of the present—of what's actually happening today in front of you—rather than dwelling on the past or worrying about the future.

»→ Give yourself permission to change your mind, ask for help, or slow down.

Affirmations for Self-Love

While your old dating mind-set might have been "Am I good enough for you?" your new mind-set should be "Are you good enough for me?" Here are some powerful affirmations that will jolt you into that more positive mind-set:

I deserve love and respect, both from myself and from a partner.

All that matters is that I feel enough for me.

My value doesn't decrease based on someone's inability to see my worth.

If they make me question my worth, they are not worthy of my love.

MEET YOURSELF

Now that you've set a foundation of love for yourself and dispelled the stories that aren't true about you, it's time to find out what *is* true. This is your opportunity to start fresh in your love life, with a blank slate about who you are. Close your eyes for a minute and imagine that you're standing in front of a big whiteboard covered in all of the major qualities, values, and accomplishments that have described you and your behaviors in the past. What adjectives stand out? Which items make you most proud? What descriptors would you like to change? Which experiences are you ready to let go of? Staring at this imaginary board, do you get an overwhelmingly positive, negative, or neutral feeling? Now, imagine yourself picking up a dry eraser and wiping away all of the preconceived notions about who you are and what you value. You're reading this book for a reason. Something, or many things, have not been working for you, so I want you to do your best to start from scratch at this point. Assume you know nothing about yourself. The remaining part of this step will help you get crystal clear on who you are and who you want to be. It's with this new identity that you can move forward to cultivate the dating life you desire, knowing and believing firmly in who you are. It is also a good idea to get feedback from those closest to you, since we don't always see ourselves the way we are perceived. Ask some of your besties what they love about you, and what they think are your best qualities or attributes that you can bring to a romantic relationship. Ask them what they admire most about your personality, mind, and body, and accept these compliments gracefully, without refuting or diminishing any feedback.

EXPLORE AND EXPERIMENT

Part of becoming an expert on yourself requires you to explore and experiment with who you are at your core. After all, how can you show up fully in your love life to let someone get to know you if *you* don't even know you? No need for an existential crisis! Let's devote time now to figure out what you care about, what kind of person you want to be, and what you want your life to look like so you can figure out who you want to share it with.

Values

It's essential to explore yourself on a deeper level by getting familiar with your core values. We all have values, but core values are the ones that are the most important and define how you want to live your life. So before you say "family" and skip right over this section, I urge you to explore even deeper about what this means to you, and revisit your values even if you already think you know what they are. For example, do your choices actually support that family is number one, or do you tend to choose your friends, career, or a passion project over seeing your parents or spending time with your siblings? Core values aren't right or wrong, and the values that influenced you as a child may no longer resonate with the lifestyle you've cultivated. Your values may shift with time and age. Something that may have really mattered to you in your twenties may no longer seem relevant in your fifties. Don't feel guilty about your values and priorities, just get real with yourself so that you can figure out what matters most. This is the perfect time to reflect and reevaluate.

    I've worked with a lot of couples who got together because of superficial qualities, such as sharing a friend group or having hot sex, but ultimately they held one or more conflicting core values, which led to resentment and ultimately the end of their partnership. This is why it's so insanely important to be an expert on yourself, so that you can choose a partner who has core values that align with yours. This will allow you to create a shared vision for the future. It's the pragmatic side of love.

Compromise is an important skill in any relationship, but you should never have to compromise on your core values. You're in the perfect position right now as a single woman because you get to choose your partner based on what matters most to you. You're not already married or committed to someone, so there's no pressure or guilt about having invested time and energy into a relationship and feeling forced to make it work despite your clashing core values. Your love life is a blank slate; make it work for you.

Below are core value questions to consider. Read through them and check off the ones that stand out as being the most meaningful to you (and of course feel free to write in your own). As with the last exercise, physically checking off these values is more meaningful than just reading through the list, so please do this for yourself. You'll know something is a core value when you know that by compromising on the topic, it violates the way you want to live—this then becomes a deal breaker.

- What are your political beliefs? Where do you fall on the liberal-to-conservative continuum?

- Do you want children? If you already have kids, do you want more with a new partner? What are your parenting philosophies? Do you want your kids to have a very similar or different upbringing than you did?

- How important is your race and culture? What, if any, issues do you foresee dating someone of a different race or culture?

- Are you health conscious? In what ways do you prioritize a healthy lifestyle? What do you do for exercise? Do you have any dietary preferences or restrictions?

- How do you manage stress? What do you do for self-care?

- Does religion or spirituality play a role in your life? Do you believe in God? How do you feel about dating some-one of a different religion or spiritual orientation?

- What level of education do you have? What values do you have around education, learning, and your degree?

- What do "family values" mean to you? How close are you to your family and how involved are they in your life?

- What are your money management practices? What types of things do you splurge on and what types of things do you save for? Do you have debt?

- Are you career-focused? What's your work-life balance? Do you prioritize work or your hobbies? Where do you fall on the scale, with 1 = lacking ambition and direction and 10 = extremely driven and professionally motivated?

- Do you value spending time in nature and the outdoors? Are you passionate about animals and pets?

- What are your sexual preferences? How often do you like to have sex when you're in a committed partnership?

- Do you volunteer? What charities, causes, or organiza-tions do you support? In what ways do you want to make the world a better place?

- How much does your physical environment contribute to your happiness? Do you prefer urban or rural living? What size house do you want to live in?

Whether you're passionate about protecting endangered animals, attending weekly Sunday-night family dinners, saving money for a house, earning your next promotion, traveling to every continent, or getting your PhD, only you can define your core values. Your dating criteria and deal breakers will be based on your core values.

Hobbies

Another part of becoming an expert on yourself is figuring out your passions, hobbies, and interests. This can be a daunting or stressful exploration for some people since there is so much pressure in our society to "brand" ourselves and declare our passions loudly. There's no hurry here; take your time, breathe deeply, and remember that there's no pressure or box to fit into.

What brings you joy? Think back to when you were a kid. You fiddled with toys, used your imagination, created artwork, enjoyed venturing outside, and maybe even participated in community organizations, such as dance, sports, and summer camp. Yet somehow as we grow up, we trade in all of this play for the daily grind at work, squeeze in a quick workout for health purposes, and grab dinner or drinks with a friend if we're lucky. Where did *play* go?

When someone asks you, "What do you do for fun?" how do you respond? Does your answer bring a smile to your face? Now is the perfect time to get reacquainted with your inner child and start exploring old and new hobbies. Sign up for guitar lessons or a foreign language, buy a cookbook and try all of the recipes, attend a new fitness class (how about aerial yoga or kickboxing?), register for a race, join a kickball league (my friend met her husband while reffing a league he played in), take a creative writing or glass-blowing workshop, or plan the international vacation of your dreams. Make no mistake—exploring hobbies is something you are doing for yourself. But a side benefit is that talking about hobbies is one of the most natural ways to spark connection and discover commonalities, and thus ends up making great date conversation later on. (Plus, having a wide variety of interests shows that you're a passionate person with a full life, which is attractive to a partner because they want to join in on the fun and expand their own world with you.)

This is the time to get out of your comfort zone and push yourself to grow. Sometimes we get stuck in a rut and don't even realize there's a different way to live. We fall into comfortable routines and walk familiar paths. Let's shake things up a bit, shall we? Try taking the opposite approach to how you normally do things. Say "yes" to every social invitation for the next two weeks. Wear an outfit that you're unsure if you can pull off and see how it feels. Hit up a different café for your morning coffee run. Instead of reaching for your phone first thing when you wake up, take a few quiet minutes to meditate.

CHOOSE YOURSELF

Before you choose a romantic partner, you must choose yourself. Make yourself a priority. You have the rest of your life to balance your needs with someone else's, so now is the time to be selfish and focus solely on you. In healthy relationships with interdependence, you'll maintain your identity, so you must figure out who you are. Choose what lights your soul on fire, what fills you up, what moves you, what gives you meaning and purpose. Set new goals based on your core values and the hobbies you want to explore. We get to define and redefine ourselves every single day, no matter our age or life situation. We do this through our actions, so make sure your choices align with who you want to be. You are defined by what *you* love, not by who loves you. Your value doesn't increase by someone wanting to date you, or by trying to be like someone else in order to seek approval or attention. You choose what's cool, sexy, and fun, so be conscious of where your influences and opinions stem from. When you honor yourself, you'll attract someone who sees, values, and supports all of you.

Ultimately you are investigating yourself for your own benefit, but the truth is that the more interests you have, the more interesting you'll be on a date. Your passions will inspire and attract others. If you want to attract a high-quality partner, you have to demonstrate that you're a high-quality person. What, you might ask, does "high-quality" mean? It doesn't mean that you're the hottest person in the room or the wealthiest; being a high-quality person means you have a zeal for life, you're not afraid to try new things, you're open-minded, you're confident in who you are, you're introspective and self-aware, and of course you can laugh at yourself when things don't go perfectly.

Oftentimes I chat with singles who have long wish lists for what they want their future partner to be, but they aren't showing up fully in their own life. They are falling flat and wouldn't make it onto their own list! Start by *being* the person you want to date. Be someone worth meeting. Ask yourself, "Would I like me? Would I be impressed, attracted to, and charmed by my life?" Don't be vanilla. Be dynamic. Be the salted caramel cookie fudge!

Scarcity Mentality vs. Abundance Mentality

Creating a successful dating life has a lot to do with your mind-set. Are you operating from one of scarcity and fear (e.g., *everyone good has been taken, I will never meet someone*, etc.), or abundance and hope (*I love how many options I have with online dating, I can't wait to have that feeling again that you get when you really like someone, the dates that don't work out teach me important lessons and get me closer to finding what I want*, etc.). When you engage in a scarcity mentality, you're sending out signals of fear and desperation, which will attract the wrong partners or repel people who may be right for you. If you want to be with a high-quality, committed partner who loves you reciprocally, then your thoughts must align with your desires. Since your thoughts impact your mood and behaviors, they create your reality. Imagine what it feels like to experience the epic love that you crave. Picture yourself laughing, cuddling, or enjoying a meal with this person. Go about your day holding this warm, loving feeling in mind, as though you're already receiving this extraordinary love. This is abundant thinking. When you think positively, you give off good energy, and the people around you will feel good and relaxed. This will, in turn, make them want to be around you more, so thinking positively serves a dual purpose.

MAKE YOURSELF

You've chosen who you are and what you want to be. Now it's time to take action and turn your thoughts into reality. Sometimes getting started can feel like the most overwhelming part, so don't forget that it's okay to take small daily steps. You don't decide to lose twenty pounds and wake up the next day having lost it. You commit to lifestyle changes, such as replacing your fast-food lunch with a salad, taking the stairs instead of the elevator, and going to a barre class instead of the bar. You can apply this approach to any goal, breaking it down into smaller, measurable actions. When you decide to make yourself, aim for a few small goals, and one or two larger goals. Do you need to have a five- or ten-year life plan? Absolutely not, but you'll feel better about yourself when you have some clear direction and create a sense of purpose. It's about setting yourself up for success and choosing to be an all-star at whatever you do.

Short-Term Goals

Short-term goals are those that you'd like to achieve in the near future, whether that's today, next week, or within the year. They can stand on their own, or tie into a larger long-term goal. Below are examples and how to achieve them:

»→ If you want to be well-read or improve your intellectual curiosity, commit to reading one book per month. To hold yourself accountable, consider joining or starting a book club. You can ask friends or post on social media for suggested books so that you're introduced to new literature. Make it fun by discussing the books with those who recommended them once you've finished reading. Keep a list of everything you've read so that you can check each book off, which is a great visual way to feel accomplished.

»→ If you want to keep a cleaner house, commit to doing one tidying act per day. This could be making your bed each morning, placing your dishes directly in the dishwasher instead of letting them pile up in the sink, or squeegeeing the shower after each use. Personally, I like to reward myself for cleaning by waiting to watch my favorite TV show until after I'm done.

Long-Term Goals

Long-term goals require at least a year's commitment. They have the potential to significantly change your life. Working toward these goals will bring you a greater sense of purpose, and they will tell the story of what you stand for. Your achievements should make you feel proud. Below are examples of long-term goals.

»→ If you want to earn a promotion, commit to making a better impression at work. Arrive five minutes early at your desk so that when your boss walks in, you're already there. Beat a timeline by delivering the task or product early. Volunteer to take on more responsibility. Show up with a positive attitude and improve the workplace environment. Let your manager know your intentions to move up into a specific role, and ask what you need to do specifically to be considered for that role. Keep a written account of everything you've accomplished that you can present to your manager during your review period.

»→ If you want to become an award-winning biologist, set your sights on getting accepted to a top-ten graduate program. Start by strengthening your candidacy: Study your butt off and aim for a 4.0 GPA, prep for standardized tests, build professional and academic relationships so that you can get stellar recommendations, and complete an internship, thesis, or portfolio to demonstrate your skill set. Stay organized by looking ahead and writing down any major deadlines in your calendar with reminders along the way. Once you're accepted into a program, plan ahead about what internships you might need to secure in order to land a job at a top science lab, seek out additional research opportunities with influential professors, and sign up for extracurricular activities, such as attending conferences or specialized trainings.

Our actions, not just our words, create who we are. When you show up in your dating life, a potential partner will look at your goals and evaluate who you are by your accomplishments. Let's be clear: You are creating these goals for yourself—not to impress another person. Creating a life to impress another person is not the goal. That said, when you meet someone new, how do you evaluate them? You look at their choices and you compare them to your own. Naturally, anyone you meet will try to gauge whether your goals align well with theirs, and what kind of couple you would make. Striving for things, having direction and purpose—these are desirable qualities. And achieving your long-term goals shows that you're not afraid of commitment and hard work. When you look back at your life, what do you want it to say about you? How do you want to feel about yourself? Creating a successful life (and dating life) involves getting your words, values, and actions in alignment.

Get Good

Before you commit to a partner, commit to yourself. Do what you say you're going to do. Accountability is a valuable life skill. Share your intentions and ambitions with friends so that they can check in with you and help keep you on track. Get clear on your core values through self-reflection and dating experiences, and continue to experiment with new hobbies. Dedicate your time and energy to figuring out what thrills *you,* and then fill your life with this goodness. Don't be afraid to fail. So much of personal growth stems from failing, learning, reevaluating, and improving upon your weaknesses. Taking risks will help you figure out your likes and dislikes. If things don't go your way, you'll at least wind up with life lessons, as well as interesting or funny stories to tell on future dates.

KEY TAKEAWAYS

Congratulations on becoming an expert on yourself. Hopefully by working through this step, you have gained some clarity on your core values, gotten excited about trying out new hobbies, or made a plan to uncover new interests that will spark joy in your life. All of these things will make you feel stronger and more grounded, irrespective of what happens in your dating life. But remember, keep at it. Growing into the person you want to be is a life-long journey.

Here are your takeaways from this step:

- You have to meet yourself before you can meet the right partner.

- Let go of old labels, narratives, and shame stories that damage your self-worth—they no longer serve you.

- Don't treat your thoughts as facts; instead challenge your stinkin' thinkin' and replace automatic or ingrained thoughts with more realistic and positive ones.

- Remember that your thoughts impact your mood, influence your behaviors, and create your reality.

- Ditch your scarcity mentality, and practice abundant thinking.

- Make self-love a daily practice. This requires compassion, kindness, and the fundamental understanding that you are enough.

💜 Get clear on your core values and choose the lifestyle you want—never compromise on these.

💜 Commit to trying new hobbies and exploring interests that light your soul on fire.

💜 Identify deal breakers by asking, "What violates the way I want to live my life?"

💜 Commit to new short- and long-term goals or double down on ones you already have for maximum personal growth.

Step

2

CHOOSE WHO
YOU WANT

GREAT NEWS: *You* get to *choose* who to date! Gone are the days of sitting around waiting for someone to like or validate you, which feels like being the last kid picked for kickball. That's not what an empowered woman does. When entering into a partnership, it's a fifty-fifty agreement, which means you have half the say of whether or not you're interested. Don't be a chameleon, changing your colors based on who you're dating, or what you think they admire. Rather than wondering whether the person sitting across from you likes you, ask yourself whether or not you like them. You have the power to reject someone, too. Remember that you know who you are, you're clear on your values and the vision you have for your life. Once you've defined yourself, you'll stop searching for yourself within others. You'll be sure of when you've met the right person because you're sure of yourself. Now let's figure out exactly what you want in an ideal match so that you can date with intention and make smart choices about who has the *privilege* of your partnership.

SET YOUR PRIORITIES

It may not be the most romantic approach to finding love, but choosing your dating criteria based on core values is a practical way to set your relationship up for success. Of course you need to feel physically attracted to your partner, but basing your dating decisions solely on looks will get you a short-lived relationship. Though you may have physical preferences, such as hair color or height, think of these as bonuses, rather than requirements. For instance, a *need* is having the same political affiliations, a *want* is someone who is 6'2".

What values do you desire in a partner? Consider the core value questions from step 1. Think about your expectations and hopes for how your partner would respond to those questions. Which shared values are must-haves, and which don't seem to matter? (As with last time, physically mark up the page or write on a separate piece of paper.) I've noticed that people tend to be either too picky about superficial things, or they fail to set any criteria because they are so desperate for love and attention. Your goal *isn't* to attract *everyone*; you only want to attract those whose core values align with yours, and with whom you share a similar vision for the future.

When you value and respect yourself, you'll set firm deal breakers. A deal breaker is nonnegotiable—you won't date someone who doesn't have these same values, beliefs, or goals, no matter how dreamy they are. Compromising on core values leads to resentment, so keeping strong boundaries around your deal breakers will help you resist the hunk who will break your heart and waste your time. For example, if you desire marriage and a family, and someone says they don't want a commitment or kids, believe them.

Don't waste your time trying to prove how wonderful you are, hoping to convince them to give you want you want. If someone you're dating expresses an opinion, value, or goal that doesn't align well with yours, it's absolutely worth having a conversation to figure out whether there's any flexibility. Not all values are defining values, and not all statements are made with a lot of thought behind them, so find out where they stand if something is important to you. They may change their mind with further discussion, education, and learning how it impacts you. However, if you're at a standstill on the things that define the way you want to live your life, walk away. You can't change someone in that deep of a way.

In addition to values, consider personality traits. Some people prioritize kindness, while others care about humor. In fact, searching for a sense of humor is one of the most popular qualities that pops up on dating profiles because who doesn't love to laugh? The problem here is that there are multiple types of humor, such as sarcasm, slapstick, or witty wordplay, so what you find funny may not be funny to someone else.

Because there are no perfect people, everyone will have some less than desirable qualities, such as being stubborn, stingy, messy, moody, irresponsible, or selfish. You probably won't witness these on a first or second date, but they will creep out with time. You're then forced to make a choice—to either label certain behaviors and qualities as deal breakers, or to accept someone with their flaws and stop defining the relationship by what's lacking. Are there any partner traits that you know you can absolutely not live with? Don't forget that you're human, and therefore imperfect, too. Knowing what you're looking for will help you date with intent and be purposeful in your partner choices so that you can more quickly recognize who is a strong fit, and not waste your precious energy on people who aren't right for you. Below are some defining traits. Which ones do you gravitate toward and why? What do they mean or represent to you? (As with the questions in step 1, check off the ones that are most important to you.)

▦	Generous	▦	Graceful
▦	Outgoing	▦	Practical
▦	Calm	▦	Intellectual
▦	Energetic	▦	Imaginative
▦	Confident	▦	Quiet
▦	Opinionated	▦	Resourceful
▦	Creative	▦	Sophisticated
▦	Warmhearted	▦	Relaxed
▦	Cheerful	▦	Active
▦	Driven	▦	Independent
▦	Cultured	▦	Moral
▦	Optimistic	▦	Artistic
▦	Adventurous	▦	Sensitive
▦	Resilient	▦	Quick-witted
▦	Sarcastic	▦	Athletic

BE OPEN TO SURPRISES.

Know what you want, but don't be so rigid in your expectations that you're closed off to anyone who isn't exactly what you envisioned. Does their specific job matter, or the fact that they're passionate about their career matter more? Does your soul mate need to be an equally accomplished triathlete, or is it okay to enjoy other fitness activities? You may not have pictured being with someone who has debt, but can you bend your rules if it's for someone responsibly paying off student loans or a mortgage, rather than a large credit card bill? Sometimes outward credentials don't always reflect actual abilities or talents, so it's up to you to determine what you value most.

I almost ruled out my husband before going on a first date because in an early message exchange I learned that he'd never been out of the country and I love international travel. He'd also never been hiking, and I love the outdoors. I was a bit turned off by both pieces of news and wondered whether we had enough shared interests to warrant a connection. I agreed to meet him despite these things, and it was the best decision I ever made. Though he didn't have the same life experiences as me, he was extremely open and enthusiastic to trying "my" activities, and I learned to play golf with him. Now we enjoy all these pastimes together. I share this with you because I could have easily assumed that since he didn't have experience with travel or the outdoors, he didn't like those activities and wasn't right for me. But I couldn't have predicted that his willingness to try and his positive attitude would be such a turn-on.

Being open can manifest in other ways, too. Be open to the package your person might come in—you may not know their size, shape, or hair color (they could be bald!), but what you do know is that powerful love is out there for you. Look past a bad haircut, a perfume or cologne you can't stand, and the ugly shirt you wish they'd throw out. Part of being open to surprises is having faith that the love of your life is out there, that there are ample dating opportunities, and that the universe is working in your favor, even when it feels like it's out to get you. This is the power of abundant thinking. Abundant thinking is about relaxing and understanding that there's enough happiness and positive outcomes out there to go around, even if it doesn't happen on the exact timeline you've laid out for your life. Just because all of your friends are married, doesn't mean that "all the good ones are taken"—because there's no scarcity of quality people. If you're constantly thinking about what you don't want, then living in this negativity will just manifest your fears and anxieties—dating duds, cheaters, rejections, and breakups—every time. You can choose to focus on what's going wrong, or you can choose to focus on putting good juju out there, exerting positive energy into the world in the form of kindness, generosity, and giving people a chance. You get back what you put out, so if you open yourself up to new experiences and different people, you may be surprised to fall for someone you may have typically written off prematurely.

UNDERSTAND YOUR ATTACHMENT STYLE

Sometimes we choose wrong. We get hurt, or we don't like who we are in a relationship and end up sticking it out with someone who brings out the worst in us. We self-sabotage and push someone away, or we cling on despite knowing we aren't being treated the way we deserve.

One major underlying factor for why you may keep choosing the wrong partners is that you're attracted to someone with a conflicting attachment style. Your attachment style is the way you relate to others. It shows itself in the ways you express (or don't express) desire, as well as your level of comfort with closeness and intimacy. It's how your brain processes whether someone feels like they are a safe person who is available and able to meet your needs. The tricky thing about attachment styles is that they form in early childhood and are primarily based on whether your caregiver was responsive and consistent in caring for you.

There are three main types of attachment styles: secure, anxious, and avoidant. It's possible for your style to shift with different life experiences and in different relationships, but some people have to work hard to understand and overcome emotional obstacles that their attachment style presents. As with most things, the first step is to acknowledge which attachment style you have and honestly analyze how your behaviors and emotions relate to it.

Singles with a secure style operate from a foundation of believing they are worthy of love, value, and respect. They're trusting, comfortable with closeness, and communicate well about relationship issues. Ideally, it's your goal in dating to both model a secure attachment and find a partner with a secure attachment, since this usually translates into healthy relationship dynamics. However, you can still find love and have a happy relationship if you're anxious or avoidant, you just have to be aware of your patterns and when you're feeling triggered.

If you have an anxious style, you desperately want to be loved, constantly worry your partner will leave you, and struggle with feelings of worthiness. In general, you feel needy, jealous, and insecure, and you second-guess behaviors, overanalyze communication, and feel on edge until your partner reassures you that the relationship is safe. There are a lot of highs, lows, and drama.

If you have an avoidant style, you want love, but you prioritize your independence, so there's a push-and-pull dynamic where you keep your partner at an arm's length physically and emotionally. You avoid true intimacy and worry about losing yourself within the relationship. You shut down when you feel like your partner needs more from you than you can provide, and you struggle to communicate about your feelings and where the relationship is heading. There's even another type of attachment style called the fearful-avoidant, which is someone who is high on both traits of avoidance and anxiety.

Unfortunately, anxious and avoidant styles are drawn together like magnets because they validate each other's unhealthy and long-standing framework that people will not meet their needs. In general, humans tend to attract those that confirm our old, shameful beliefs (the stories we tell ourselves), and it's no different here. If we think we're unworthy of love, we attract those who can't commit or who will leave us. If we think people are controlling, smothering and won't give us autonomy, we attract those that seem needy, jealous, and fearful. We tend to push away people who contradict our beliefs about what we deserve, so we wind up dating the same person in a different body every time. The anxious person wants closeness and validation and comes off as insecure, and the avoidant person wants space and freedom, and comes off as belittling and distant. Do you keep picking someone who activates your attachment system?

You'll want to take attachment styles into account when choosing a partner. Even if someone has all of the personality traits and values you're looking for, if you're highly anxious and they're horrible at communication, give you mixed signals about commitment, or struggle to show you the affection and attention you asked for (signs of an avoidant), they're probably not going to be a great partner for you, and will constantly activate your attachment system. On the flip side, if you're avoidant, you may find that an anxiously attached partner feels overbearing and controlling, so you may do better with someone secure who won't have a total meltdown when you need a bit of space. The right partner can help you heal old wounds and provide a safe and secure emotional home while you're committed to self-improvement work.

KEY TAKEAWAYS

This step is all about empowering you to believe that you get to choose your ideal match, rather than waiting around to be picked. You're a conscious, intentional dater, which means you're falling for someone *not* because of how attractive they are, or an initial spark, but because there are substantial traits and shared core values that support long-term relationship success. Here are your key takeaways:

💜 Choose your dating criteria based on core values, shared goals, and personality traits, not sex appeal.

💜 Set firm deal breakers and walk away when you come across the things that violate the way you want to live your life.

💜 Identify the personality qualities of an ideal match, but realize there are no perfect people, so you will have to accept their imperfections as well.

💜 Don't worry about attracting everyone; there's an abundance of singles out there who will align with your desires.

💜 Be open to surprises and the unknown package in which your partner will come.

💜 Understand your attachment style and when your anxious or avoidant system is activated; strive to model secure behaviors.

HOW TO MEET SOMEONE WORTHY OF YOUR TIME AND WHAT TO DO WHEN IT HAPPENS

THERE ARE TWO main ways to meet people today: online and IRL (in real life). In either case, you need to be vulnerable, confident, and put yourself out there to create a meaningful connection. Let's first dive into some online dating strategy, and then look at how to be approachable and how to approach someone who catches your eye in the wild.

ADVICE ON DATING APPS AND SOCIAL MEDIA

Online dating and dating apps have the biggest ROI (return on investment) in your dating life since they're tools that help you connect with hundreds, if not thousands, of other singles—and all from the convenience of your own home. According to researchers at Match, meeting online is the number one way singles connect today, with more than half of U.S. singles having tried online dating or dating apps. Beyond that, the average dater uses three apps at a time. So if you're a late adopter, it's time to hop on the bandwagon.

It's worth noting that social media is also playing an increasing role in how people meet, whether it's "sliding into your DMs" on Instagram, or a comment on Facebook that sparks a connection. There's even an article on Thrillist.com that discusses how any app, such as Yelp, Goodreads, Sound-Cloud, or Venmo, can be a dating app if you try hard enough. People fantasize and get so attached to an ideal "how we met" story that they miss real opportunities to connect. If that's you, realize that it doesn't matter how you meet, as long as this person makes their way into your life.

Regardless of how the apps and sites are marketed, they all host a variety of daters who are somewhere on the continuum of looking for a casual hookup to searching for a lifelong partner. Hot tip: Those who have left the content of their profile blank, only have one or two photos, and who are overtly sexual in their messaging are clearly not looking for a serious commitment, so keep an eye out for those red flags. Instead focus on those who have taken the time to create a thoughtful, creative profile, with bonus points for couple-oriented language, or a statement about seeking a relationship.

Your goal with online dating is to quickly figure out if you're attracted to their photos, if they seem to have a good personality, and if you share any mutual interests, values, or goals. Based on their pictures and written profile content, and a few back-and-forth messages, you need to decide whether you want to meet IRL. Online dating should be used in a similar way to when you see a hottie at the bar and you suss them out with a short convo before exchanging numbers. You don't need to know their whole life story or what they're looking for, since you wouldn't have this info when approaching at the bar; so use their profile and a few messages as a tool to decide whether you're attracted to them, then arrange a time to meet and go from there. This should take a day or week at most; you don't want a long-term pen pal. At this point, you're not evaluating whether they have all of your must-have criteria but simply whether they're worth an hour of your time for a first date. Overall, if you like 80 percent of what you've learned about them and how they've made you feel in your short interactions, get offline and meet in person. In person is the only way to see if there's chemistry and establish a true connection.

Keep in mind that not everyone is quick-witted with banter or a talented writer, so if messaging has left you on the fence, I recommend a brief phone call to see if you're put at ease. In this day and age, many people are shy about having phone calls at all, even with people they know, so the idea of a call with a total stranger can seem daunting. Let me reassure you that it's worth a quick phone screen because you get a surprising amount of info about the other person just from hearing the tone of their voice, the way they speak, whether they have an accent, their word choice, whether they seem confident or nervous, their ability to carry a convo, what their laugh sounds like, how fast or slowly they speak, and whether they put you at ease or on edge. Make no mistake, you can definitely get a sense of chemistry over the phone. If you're not feeling their vibe, then you know with little investment that it's not a match. If they ask you on the spot whether you'd like to plan a date, and it's a firm no, simply let them know you appreciated the call, but that unfortunately you didn't feel a connection and want to be respectful of each other's time. If it feels confrontational or too much pressure, you can always send a kind but direct text a few hours later with the same message.

Since you're dating with intent, commit to being open to messaging with everyone with whom you match. Rather than swiping out of boredom or for an ego boost, this pact with yourself will cause you to be more purposeful in your choices since you're forced to pay attention to *why* you're swiping, knowing a conversation will ensue, especially if you're using one of the female-led apps, such as Bumble, which requires the woman to message first. I recommend matching and conversing with a maximum of five people at a time; otherwise it gets confusing, hard to recall specific details about each person, and you can't remember who you told what! Once you've ruled someone out, un-match and open up a slot for someone new. This will help with the mental overload. If Marie Kondo were a dating coach, she'd tell you to un-match and delete messages from people with whom you're no longer interested to minimize mental and visual clutter in your in-box. If you prefer to leave old matches so that you don't accidentally rematch with someone you previously ruled out, that's fine, too, or keep a list in a journal or on your phone that you can cross-check.

Your profile is the backbone of your personality. It's a window into who you are, what you stand for, and what you desire in a partner. This is your chance to make the best first impression possible, so there's no room for negativity, especially since many of the apps limit you to between 150 to 500 characters. Say goodbye to a list of picky partner requirements that make you seem high maintenance, or wasting characters with comments such as, "I don't really know how to describe myself." If you don't smile when writing about it, delete it. Highlight the things you love about yourself: your passions, hobbies, accomplishments, and qualities that make you unique. I shared that I never drank a cup of coffee in my life and am allergic to avocado (I know, it sucks!), which was an easy icebreaker that a lot of people sent me a lighthearted message about. Don't do the generic list of adjectives that so many singles resort to: funny, kind, athletic, foodie, nerd. These words don't differentiate you from anyone else using them. Instead, bring these traits to life with my motto, *convey it, don't say it*. Paint a picture of how you embody these qualities with little vignettes from your life. For instance, instead of "adventurous traveler" write, "Got my adrenaline fix skydiving in Australia." If you're humorous and passionate about saving the environment, you might share, "I wear socks that match and I recycle." Also, don't be afraid to show that you're serious about a relationship—this puts you in the girlfriend bucket instead of the hookup bucket. Write a statement such as, "Looking for my brunch-mate and ready to show the world what a power couple looks like," which uses couple-oriented language. Put out into the universe what you desire, and you will receive it.

In terms of photos, you must include the following three images: headshot, full body, and activity. You don't want to be one-dimensional, so include a couple of each and make sure you're in different outfits and scenes.

A headshot needs to clearly show your characteristics, so no big sunglasses or hats blocking your beautiful face. What makes a good Snapchat photo doesn't make a good dating profile pic—leave the filters, especially the animal ears, behind. I repeat: NO FILTERS OR ANIMAL EARS. If possible, it's best to show two to three headshots since it can be hard to get a full picture of what someone looks like from just one photo, so use different angles and hairstyles that you typically wear.

A full body shot is head to toe so someone can get a decent sense of your figure. Don't crop the photo so only part of your body is showing: Be proud of your shape. Only the people who are attracted to you will want to meet you, so you have nothing to worry or be self-conscious about in terms of your appearance as long as you're accurately representing yourself. If you choose a shot that doesn't accurately represent your body, you're going to be worried about the person's reaction when you meet them in person. Why make yourself nervous for no reason? Don't do this to yourself. If you get to the point of meeting someone, they are going to see what your body looks like, so don't shoot yourself in the foot by misrepresenting yourself in the beginning.

An activity photo is one of you participating in something you love, whether it's walking your pet, skiing, eating a stack of gourmet pancakes, crossing the finish line, or with a piece of art you created. Activity photos make it easy for someone to find something to message you about, plus these photos help you with the conversation, since it feels natural and exciting to talk about your passions.

When selecting photos, keep in mind that nothing is worse than showing up on a first date and being disappointed that your date looks nothing like their pics, so make sure to use recent images. The person can usually feel your disappointment, and you both end up feeling that you've wasted your time. So make sure you are not guilty of this. Have courage and integrity; represent yourself accurately, and you will find people who are doing the same.

How to Handle Unsolicited Dick Pics

According to a YouGov survey, 53 percent of millennial women have received a naked photo from a man. Match did a similar survey and found that 50 percent of women had specifically received an *unrequested* dick pic. Because there is no consent involved, getting an unrequested dick pic is, in fact, a form of sexual harassment. Take it seriously, as such. Block, report, and don't reply. Don't give him a reaction, which is likely what he's looking for. Or, if you're feeling brazen, you can try one of these funny lines from Reddit users: "Wow. That's weird looking. What did the Dr. say?" "Congratulations, my vagina has never been more dry," or send back a picture of a bigger penis, then stop engaging and block. All joking aside, it's really important to keep your safety in mind and not egg someone on who might harass you further or take it to a violent level. It's unfair that women have to curb their behaviors because of what some men do, but unfortunately that is still a reality. So if you do want to give a funny reply, err on the side of caution, and only do it in circumstances where you do not think the person will react by being violent or escalating the situation.

HOW AND WHERE TO MEET PEOPLE

You're sick of swiping left and right on the dating apps and hoping to meet someone the romantic, old fashioned, organic way—IRL. Yet, when you go out, you never seem to meet anyone, or you're with your same group of friends and can't seem to break out of your bubble. This section is going to give you some tips about how you can shake it up and start meeting new people.

Out and About

Before going out into public, you must take a few steps.

First, get in the right mind-set and ditch your pessimism. With your new abundant thinking, affirm that "there are countless high-quality, attractive people I can meet today" or "today might be the day I meet an incredible significant other."

Second, if you recognize that you're going out with the same people or to the same places all the time, break your routine. Schedule outings with different friends and to different places than you normally go. Be aware of the number of people you're planning to go out with. It's intimidating for someone to approach you in a huge group, as well as when you're intimately sitting with just one other person, so aim for a small group of three to five. If you're hanging with a guy friend, a stranger may mistake this for a date, and the same applies to same-sex orientations, so be conscious of the way you may be perceived.

Third, since you never know when and where you might meet your match, whether it's in line at the juice bar, or while boarding an airplane, treat each outing as a potential for a first encounter. That means your appearance and body language matters. What do you want to be wearing when you meet your special someone? Take pride in your appearance since it's an outward expression of your confidence. What does your body language say about you? Are you always staring into your phone when you're in public—either texting or scrolling through your social media feed? Or are you talking on it to pass the time? If so, someone might feel that they'll be interrupting you if they try to get your attention. Practice being approachable in public by looking up and assertively making eye contact with a smile. It can feel a little scary, but it's also a thrill when you have a flirty exchange with someone.

Fourth, your goal is to create as many windows of opportunity to interact with new people as possible. That means you must be ready to actually talk to people when you're out and about. Seize all situations for a connection. As we just discussed, no using your phone as a security blanket. Recognize that there's no perfect place to meet a potential partner. You could encounter your soul mate in an elevator at the mall, ordering lunch at your favorite food truck, or in line at the post office while doing your Amazon returns. My friend Jen met her husband at a coffee shop when she asked him to watch her belongings so that she could go to the bathroom. My client Grayson, 27, went on a date with a woman he met in a parking garage after he assisted her in squeezing her car into a tight spot. My 53-year-old divorced client Stella has been dating her boyfriend, Mike, for a few years after sitting next to him on Amtrak. She saw him from afar and thought he was cute—luckily the seat next to him was free and she was bold enough to sit in it. Monique, 38, met her wife at roller derby practice. They became friends and even lived together as roommates before things turned romantic. You won't find love at home in your sweatpants—well, unless you're online dating. The point is, the potential for love is all around us, but creating a successful dating life requires taking action.

To increase your chances of making a connection, brainstorm places where the type of people you share common values, interests, or hobbies with tend to gather. For instance, if you want to meet a mindful yogi, attend a wellness retreat. If you want to encounter a fellow cosplay fan, attend a Comic-Con event. If you want your very own doctor McDreamy, eat lunch in the hospital cafeteria. My 36-year-old client, Avery, recently moved to a new city and complained that she kept meeting immature "bros" who weren't looking for a commitment. When I asked her where she met her last date, she said at college football night at a local sports bar. That may be an appropriate bar for someone in their early or mid-twenties to find a hookup, but Avery was looking for marriage and kids. Instead, we brainstormed some bars and lounges that catered to a more established clientele, and I also steered her toward local activities related to fitness since she loved to work out. She ended up going on a date with a man she met at her first boxing class. Think strategically about the location, facility, and town you're going out in if you desire to meet someone of a certain socioeconomic status, education, religion, or sexual orientation.

Below are some examples of places you can meet a potential partner. Make sure to switch up the time of day and days of the week when you go to these places since people do tend to have routines, and you don't want to continually encounter the same people. And don't forget to seek out opportunities and events advertised online and through social media:

»» 5K, marathon, Spartan Race, or Tough Mudder

- A park, dog park, arboretum, or botanical garden (hang where people are most likely to gather and chat, such as near basketball or tennis courts, a baseball field, fountains, or attractions)
- Art gallery or museum
- BBQ or friend's party
- Beach, lake, or river with sand and water sports
- Bookstore, literary reading, or book club
- Charity event, auction, or volunteer opportunity
- Coffee shop, grocery store, restaurant—especially during special tasting events
- College alumni event in your city
- Comedy show or improv class
- Company-wide work event (if you work for a large enough company or one in which dating someone in another part of the organization would not cause a problem or affect your work life)
- Concert, opera, or Cirque du Soleil
- Craft show
- Educational class (cooking, language, art, music, etc.)
- First Friday (many cities have these as free block–party type events)
- Fitness class (spinning, CrossFit, boxing, kickboxing, rock climbing wall, yoga, stand-up paddle boarding)
- Group tour and group travel (it's okay to sign up solo; you'll meet people through these activities)
- Intramural sports league (there are some that are more social and less competitive)
- Lecture or educational event

- »»→ Local farmers' market
- »»→ Music festival
- »»→ Place of worship
- »»→ Professional networking event or social club with memberships
- »»→ Professional sporting event
- »»→ Salsa or swing night
- »»→ Ski lodge
- »»→ Wine tasting or brewery

Friends of Friends/Befriend the Partners of Your Friends

Before the days of social media and online dating, a friend setup was a popular way to meet a new romantic partner. And today, nothing is preventing you from tapping into this old-school way of connecting. Plus, there are benefits; these potential dates are already vouched for by people you know and trust, which diminishes the "stranger danger" feeling. Your friends are potentially sitting on a pile of gold; people in their network could be a great match for you, or at least worth one date! They could be your friends' coworkers, cousins, gym buddies, or acquaintances from their other friend groups. There's also so much value in getting to know the husbands, boyfriends, wives, and girlfriends of your friends since they can tap into their own separate networks. When a friend sets you up and makes an intro, it's an instant endorsement that you're someone worth getting to know, and this increases your appeal. Rather than having to pitch yourself, which can sometimes feel like bragging, your friend can highlight all of your amazing accomplishments and why they adore you so much. They can tailor their "pitch" to highlight what they already know you and your potential date have in common. Requesting a setup is nothing to be embarrassed about, so don't be shy or bashful about asking if anyone knows someone who could be a good fit. I once chatted with someone who told me she met her husband simply by asking her manicurist if she knew anyone single, and the connection was made! You're probably connected to way more people than you think; your match could be six degrees, or just two degrees, of separation from you right now.

WHAT TO DO WHEN YOU MEET SOMEONE YOU'RE INTERESTED IN

Asking someone out on a date requires vulnerability and confidence since there's always the chance they'll say no. If you don't approach them or make an attempt to ask them out, though, you may miss the opportunity and leave the situation the same way it started—without knowing their name or number, and without a date! When someone catches your attention, the *only* way to secure a date is to interact. Just keep in mind that when approaching a stranger, unless they have a ring on their finger, you have no idea if they're single or taken, whether they're attracted to you or not, and you don't know their sexual orientation. That means you can't let the fear of the unknown or the fear of rejection hold you back. At the end of the day, everyone likes to feel attractive, so if they are taken or they are not interested, they will still be flattered that they caught someone's attention (as long as you approach them in a respectful way). If they just aren't into you from a brief interaction, refuse to take it personally, and be proud that you put yourself out there. Don't let it bruise your ego. In fact, experiencing rejection will make you more resilient. It will strengthen your confidence when you realize that you are *totally fine* after being rejected. You'll be able to pat yourself on the back for having courage and laugh that you struck out. Operating from a foundation of self-love and knowing your worth is so important in the dating process, so any attempts that don't go your way won't shake your sense of self. And should they go your way, you may have just met your match.

Like animals in the wild, when you're on the hunt for a partner, you're judging and assessing each person through nonverbal behaviors before any conversation takes place. Based on someone's facial expressions and body posture, you instinctively ask questions and come to conclusions about what their intentions are and whether they're going to follow through with those intentions. For instance, you may wonder, "Is this person checking me out and are they going to approach me?" or "Is this person flirting with me and are they going to ask me out?" Within a matter of seconds, you make automatic decisions about whether someone feels safe, dangerous, friendly, or trustworthy, as well as how competent they are at getting what (you think) they want.

Just as you're judging this sexy stranger, they're judging you, too, which is why it's your job to give the green light signal that you're open to an interaction—if you are. If you are interested or curious, your nonverbal behaviors should be hinting that you're into it, and that you'd say "yes" to a date. The secret sauce to showing you're interested without actually saying it is something you're probably already doing every day—making eye contact and smiling. Yes, it's that simple! The problem is, when you're attracted to someone, you may get nervous. Instead of making eye contact, you may avert your eyes since you're intimidated. This sheepish behavior gives off the wrong signal and conveys disinterest. There's a big difference between making flirty eyes in the elevator and staring down at your shoes—it's your goal to create connection, so muster up the courage to bat those lashes.

To give the green light signal, take the following two steps: Make eye contact for three seconds and flash a smile. Repeat this two or three times depending on the situation since your romantic interest may have missed your green light in a busy environment, such as at a bar or crowded fitness class. When you're engaged in conversation, hold this eye contact and smile as much as possible. Laughing is a strong signal, too. This sounds simple, but in reality, making eye contact with a stranger for three seconds can feel like a long time. So get out there and practice so that you'll know what to do when the right person walks in and you're left breathless!

In a world where we're always looking down at our phones, people have forgotten how to gaze into each other's eyes. An easy way to build confidence in your eye contact is to first start by staring at yourself in the mirror (hello, beautiful!) and counting to three in your head so that you can get comfortable with how long three seconds actually lasts. Then, make sure to give yourself a big smile. Practice this every day, especially before you go out in public, since it's possible to meet a potential match any time you leave the house. Next, start making eye contact in public with people that you're *not* attracted to so that you're not consumed with the outcome of the conversation. For instance, lock eyes with a stranger that you pass by on the sidewalk when you ask to pet their cute pup. When you're in the checkout line at the grocery store, look the cashier in their eyes and casually ask how their day is going.

Since making eye contact and smiling can also just be the signs of a friendly person, if you *are* attracted to someone, you have to take it one step further to make sure you're not giving off friend-zone vibes. Practice these different types of interactions, and notice how you act and what you feel internally during both kinds. When you're chatting with someone you're interested in, you can amp up your flirtatious energy by

Have Wingwomen

My hope for you is that you feel self-assured and confident enough to go out and do things on your own. However, it can be more fun to have wingwomen by your side who help you socialize and force you out of your comfort zone. Plus, research shows that due to something called the "cheerleader effect," women in groups are sometimes deemed more attractive compared to when they're alone since your brain averages out all of the faces in a group setting and counterbalances any unattractive qualities. As mentioned, make sure to go out with three to five friends, since an admirer may not want to barge into a situation where you're intimately talking one-on-one with a friend, or they may feel unnerved to approach a big group.

This part is tricky, but it needs to be said. If you are out specifically looking to make a romantic connection, consider the friends you are with and make sure it's those who will help you foster a connection, not drive one away or steal the show. I know it's not nice to think about, but the truth is that there are some types of friends who can inadvertently kill your pickup abilities: friends who upstage you because they have a dominant energy or have performative personalities. This is NOT a reason to stop seeing your friends who you adore, but rather an opportunity to honestly evaluate who you are surrounding yourself with when you're specifically going out with the intention to make a romantic connection.

thinking a seductive thought to yourself while sustaining eye contact. For example, think, *I know I'm attractive, I know you want me*, or *You can't resist me*, which may cause you to crack a mischievous smile and give you that extra boost of confidence. You want the sexual tension to build so much that you can both feel it strongly. Practice these self-affirming thoughts in the mirror and notice the energy it brings to your body.

Speaking of your body, be aware of your posture. Are you standing tall and self-assured, or slouched with crossed arms? Do you have an RBF (resting bitch face) or are you laughing and approachable? Are you easily accessible, or closed off in the corner with your back to the door? When you're out, position yourself in ways that are inviting and welcoming: At the coffee shop, face the door and grab a table near the line where people will be passing by; in a yoga class, place your mat in the center of the studio so that people can work out on either side of you; at the bar, choose a corner seat so that you can maximize the number of people surrounding you. When you see someone you're attracted to, physically stand or sit near them, or make it a point to walk past them even when there is a more convenient way to get from point A to point B. Then lock eyes and smile to make sure they notice you.

Now that you have the nonverbals down, let's explore what to say to break the ice that won't leave you stumbling over your words or feeling too cheesy. It's helpful to use a "hostess of the party" mentality. When you're the hostess of an event, it's your job to introduce yourself, greet strangers, and make them feel comfortable and welcome. Take this role into the real world and exude this hostess energy in every social situation. An ice-breaker should be natural and contextual to what you're doing. You don't have to rack your brain too hard, just start with a simple question or comment. For example, if you see a cutie at the grocery store, say, "Hi, do you know how to tell if this fruit is ripe?" or "Any idea how to cook this?" If it's an activity, such as a gym class, ask someone if they've done it before or how to do it, or give them a compliment about what they're doing. It doesn't need to be brilliant: "It looks like you really know what you're doing!" or "Looks like you've had some practice, how long will it take me to be able to do that/lift that/look like that?" Pair this with a big smile, and it's enough to get the ball rolling. At the bar, ask for a drink suggestion, or ask the hottie what they're drinking. When you're at a total loss for words and can't think of anything witty, step into that hostess mentality and say hi, then stick out your hand and introduce yourself. It's simple, and it works. This instantly breaks the touch barrier and opens the conversation to potential flirty comments, such as, "Well don't you have a firm handshake!" or "That's a beautiful name." You can always let the other person pick up the slack if you're tongue-tied. Keep in mind that gender differences exist with pickup lines. Studies show that women prefer openers that are innocuous and hide a person's intentions, likely because it makes them feel safe and there's no overt sexual pressure. However, men appreciate direct openers, such as, "I'm shy, but I noticed you sitting here and I just had to come say hello and get to know you" or "I think you're really handsome, are you single?" Either way, if the person is single and attracted to you, a conversation is likely to happen. If that feels a little too bold, just stick with a neutral opener and see if he takes the bait. After all, the thrill of the chase is *real*!

How to Get the Date

The key to closing the deal is to be casually confident, but not aggressive. Before you jump right into asking someone on a date, butter them up—genuinely, of course—with a compliment since we tend to like people who like us. Try to make it something with substance or that will make them feel special.

Whether you meet at a friend's party, charity event, or book signing, you can say something such as: "It's so refreshing to talk to someone who cares about . . ."; "I'm really impressed with your knowledge of . . ."; "I love how passionate you are about . . ."; "I'm really drawn to how you . . ."; "It's not every day that I meet someone who . . ."; "I love how you just . . ."; "Wow, you have great taste in . . ." Even if your interactions are minimal, you can still compliment their taste in a food or drink selection, their abilities that you observed in a class, or if all else fails, their appearance, something they're wearing, their smile, or a unique feature (a guy at a bar once told me my lisp was adorable and I was instantly hooked). See if they offer a compliment in return, or make a statement about how enjoyable it's been talking to you, which is a positive sign that they're into you. At this point, they may step up and ask *you* out.

Another approach to try out is to insert a little sarcasm or playfulness, which is one form of flirting. Think about your favorite romcom or drama and how quick-witted the "meeting" scenes are. What is it exactly that creates an epic back-and-forth exchange that seems so smooth, intense, and effortless all at the same time? Sometimes that initial desire and attraction comes from not knowing how a situation will play out. Sexual tension is built on unspoken attraction, flirtation, and being a little mysterious (note: these game-like interactions may be enticing for a first encounter, but clear communication and expressing your feelings are required to build an ongoing relationship). In reality, the majority of us aren't movie stars, and these types of quick-banter encounters are a fantasy. By holding out for this type of interaction, you're probably missing out on real opportunities to talk to other humans. Often your first interactions with someone are a little awkward or funny or nerve-racking, and this is a good thing! This is the exciting, thrilling, heart-pounding stuff that you'll likely laugh about later together. With that said, if you want to try leading with a little sass, keep the following in mind: Sometimes it's not so much what you say but how you say it. If you're wildly attracted to someone that's hitting on you, you may tease, "I'm not impressed, you'll have to try harder" with a coy smile that lets them know you want them to continue talking to you. If someone asks for your number, you might joke, "I'm still on the fence, tell me why I should give you a chance" with a wink, or if they ask you on a date but you need to feel them out a bit more, you might say, "If you play your cards right!" You might even tease them in a carefree way about the terrible reasons why you could never date them, which only puts in their head the idea of dating you. This approach can be a fun way to flirt and intensifies the "hunt" for a man, so don't be afraid to experiment with your style and see what feels authentic and comfortable for you. All that said, if you are interested, make sure you're clearly conveying this even if you are jokingly challenging them. Don't go too far by being overtly mean or standoffish, which is really just a defense mechanism to avoid vulnerability. It will backfire. It will either send mixed signals that will cause them to back off, or you could hurt their pride, or they could perceive that you are a cruel or immature person. No one wants to be with someone who is mean, so if you find yourself flirting by being mean (this is called "negging"), check yourself and change course. Negging is essentially the same thing as when the boy on the playground is mean to the girl he likes. Perhaps it's cute for children, but in adults, it's usually the sign of someone who is not very emotionally evolved.

If you're doing the pursuing, a natural place to insert your ask is to reference something you chatted about or bonded over, then say you'd love to continue the convo over drinks or coffee. An easy format is "Would you like to continue to talk about our mutual like/dislike/passion for XYZ over drinks next week?" For example, imagine you asked for someone's opinion about what to order at a café, which led to a spontaneous conversation while waiting in line. You might say, "Well, you're quite the coffee connoisseur! I'd love to learn more about you over a cup another time if you're interested." They will either say yes or no. Depending on their answer, you can either exchange numbers or wish them a good day and move on. No matter what happens, always leave with your head held high.

Perhaps someone caught your eye at the gym and you've done some light chatting or tend to exchange casual pleasantries whenever you see them, but you haven't had the courage to explore a romantic connection. You could say, "We never have a chance to talk since I'm always rushing to get my workout in, would you like to grab a smoothie or drink sometime outside of the gym?" Suggest a different environment from where you typically see them, which implies it's a date versus just another friendly encounter. Also, rather than extend your time together right then and there, suggest to meet in the future so that you can create anticipation for the date. Or you can try a straightforward approach, such as, "This was fun, want to go on a date sometime?" In the chance someone says no, you have nothing to be embarrassed about, so don't apologize. Remember that at the very least they will likely be flattered by your attempt, so don't feel awkward or ashamed—you are bold, confident, and have some serious guts.

One last thing to be aware of when approaching someone is the common mistake of overstaying your welcome, especially when they look visibly uncomfortable or the conversation isn't flowing naturally. Don't be pushy or try to force it. Pay attention to their body language. Read their signals. And be aware that different contexts will warrant different lengths of conversation. For instance, introducing yourself to a stranger at the bar who is with their group of friends should be a much shorter exchange than striking up conversation with someone at a friend's intimate dinner party. Always err on the side of leaving someone wanting more. When you step away, see if they find a reason to re-initiate with you. No matter the outcome of your approach, remember that you are fabulous, and walk away with some swagger in your step.

As with all of my advice, think of these approach-techniques as guidelines or suggestions, rather than steadfast rules. If you tend to be passive and shy, and fantasize a lot about the things you wish you said or did, try being more direct and assertive. See how empowering it can be. Being more assertive has a funny way of getting you what you want! On the contrary, if you have a powerful personality, you may come across as too dominant or alpha, especially when you're nervous and trying to force something to happen. This can be the case for a lot of high-powered women who often live in their "masculine" energy, killing it as total bosses at work, but being too "bossy" in their love lives by night. You don't have to be submissive or a pushover to find someone. I am not encouraging you to change your personality. (Please don't!) If you are an assertive person, your ideal match will love how you take charge (again, *never* dumb yourself down or dim your bright light). But keep in mind that it's okay, and often necessary to soften and allow yourself to be led, pursued, and courted. If you constantly find yourself initiating, try a mental reframe that waiting for him to initiate isn't coming from a place of weakness, but rather it's a gift you can give a man to let him pursue you. I know that an empowered woman doesn't want to hear about traditional gender roles, but when it comes to dating, in all of my personal and client experiences, there's something to be said for letting the man hunt. So stand firmly in your worth, but try giving it a little more time than you normally would to see if he steps up and takes action. Every relationship has a push and pull, so you want to demonstrate that you are a flexible person who is not so one-note—especially at the beginning. Doing this is not "changing your personality" or "betraying yourself."

When someone is attracted to you, you'll know it because they will find reasons to approach you, and ask you out, so give them the time and space to step up. If you tend to control everything, such as the pace of the conversation or the speed at which a relationship moves, get out of your head and into your body; allow yourself to receive. As a big personality myself, it felt so nice to finally let go a bit and allow my partner to take the lead so I didn't have to worry about planning everything all of the time. We actually joked about this before our first date because I kept trying to coordinate all of the details, and he said, "Let me do this."

If what you've been doing hasn't been working, think about making these tweaks and helpful changes. At the end of the day, having a thriving dating life is all about presenting your best self, but it's also about being authentically you, so if the suggestions in this chapter just aren't for you, that's all right, too. If that means you are quirky and slightly awkward, someone out there will find you absolutely a*dork*able, so you do you, girlfriend! Just own it and don't stress about saying the perfect thing, since no such thing exists.

KEY TAKEAWAYS

You now have a foundation for an online dating strategy, as well as how to attract a sexy stranger and land a date in the wild. Remember to consciously choose abundant thoughts—that it's possible to meet your match any day or time you leave your house. Here are your step 3 takeaways:

💜 The purpose of online dating and apps is to get offline and meet in person, so if you're jazzed by 80 percent of someone's profile, meet IRL.

💜 Watch for red flags, such as a blank profile, minimal photos, and overtly sexual messaging.

💜 Take time to create a thoughtful profile that stands out from the rest and comes to life when using the *convey it, don't say it* motto, as well as using three to six images that include a headshot, full body, and activity photo.

💜 Tap into your friend and extended networks for a setup, and think strategically about where your ideal match would hang out.

💜 Use your "hostess of the party" mentality to confidently approach and ask someone out, and remember that rejections won't kill you. In fact, they'll make you more resilient!

💜 Be aware of your facial expressions and nonverbal behaviors. Practice smiling and eye contact, which are the green light signals that you're interested and approachable.

💜 An icebreaker should be a natural, contextual question, comment, or suggestion based on your environment.

💜 Offer a genuine compliment, try flirting with playfulness, and seal the deal with an ask such as, "Would you like to continue to talk about our mutual like/dislike/passion for XYZ over drinks next week?"

Step

4

HOW TO BE SUCCESSFUL ON A FIRST DATE

OSCAR WILDE'S famous quote "Be yourself; everyone else is already taken" couldn't be a more appropriate dating motto. In step 1 you figured out who you are. In steps 2 and 3, you looked outward. Next is step 4, which is about embracing your individuality with fierce confidence so you can slay your date. Let's dive into how to foster confidence on a date, which requires self-compassion, vulnerability, and permission to not be perfect.

GETTING READY:
MENTAL AND PHYSICAL PREP

Before heading out for a date, you must get in the right mind-set by tapping into your powerful, confident energy. Your mental prep will help you project your best self and not get so hung up on the outcome of your date. This will help you be in the moment and actually enjoy yourself. After all, dating should be fun! Here are three ways to mentally and physically get in the right mind-set for a date.

Your first exercise is to **turn any date anxiety into excitement**. So how do you shift that knot in your stomach into something pleasurable? It comes down to understanding that nervousness stems from the same brain region as excitement; it's just how you perceive and respond to the situation that alters it from a negative to a positive emotion. Both of these intense arousal states are felt in the anticipation of an event. To put this in different words: Anxiety and excitement are basically the same thing—just with different outcome expectations attached. They are two sides of the same coin, and thus it is much easier to turn one into the other than you may think.

Anxiety is triggered when something feels out of your control or uncertain, with the potential for an undesirable outcome—in this case meeting a stranger and knowing you're going to be evaluated by them on your date. When dating, there can be all sorts of automatically perceived threats that trigger anxiety, such as your physical safety, someone standing too close or leaning in for a kiss, an unpleasant memory of your ex popping into your head, saying or doing something embarrassing, or "failing" to get a second date. Anxiety research has found that this emotion can lower your self-confidence, which profoundly influences decision-making and behavior. This is why you may do or say something disingenuous on a date in the hopes of approval—or why you may not be able to say anything at all if you're stuck in a fight-flight-freeze state. When you're feeling anxious, you're likely to focus on the possible negative outcomes of the date and believe these outcomes are more likely to occur. Remember, your automatic thoughts impact your mood, behavior, and reality. The good news is that preperformance date anxiety can be managed—and transformed into excitement. Anxiety research by Alison Brooks of Harvard Business School shows that rather than trying to calm down, people who are able to transform their anxiety into excitement actually tend to feel more excited and perform better. Researchers have also found that when you're excited, you tend to view the potential for a positive outcome as more likely.

You can turn your anxiety into excitement easily before a date with a super simple self-talk strategy. Try writing "Get excited!" on a sticky note and pasting it on your mirror so you see it while you're getting ready. Or you can simply say "I'm excited" out loud a few times before walking into your date (. . . maybe do this at home so people on the street don't look at you funny). Whatever your strategy, telling yourself repeatedly that you're excited ahead of time can help you look forward to the date, show up with a more open attitude, and envision a positive outcome. Psychologists at the University of Kansas explored how smiling helps us recover from stress and found that forcing a smile can indeed reduce stress and lower our heart rates in tense situations. Smiling releases neurotransmitters such as dopamine, which increases serotonin (and causes happy feelings!), which lowers feelings of stress and depression. So smiling when you're in a bad mood can actually shift your mood. You might think doing something as simple or seemingly silly as telling yourself that you're excited won't work, but science tells us otherwise.

Your second exercise to increase confidence before a date is to **strike a Wonder Woman pose**. Expansive body posture has been shown to make us feel more powerful, perform better in interviews, and actually increase our testosterone and decrease our cortisol (the stress hormone). These poses have been shown to affect people of all genders, but have been particularly effective for women, who have been socialized to make themselves physically small and meek, as discussed in step 1. To reap these benefits before a date, stand in front of the mirror for two minutes in a power pose with your hands on your hips and your chest high and open. Or stretch your arms and legs out, with as wide a stance as you can manage and try to reach the sky, using your energy to make yourself as big as possible. Take up as much space as you can. Feel your energy pulsing outwards, in all of your poised confidence. You are striking, magnetic, and a total badass! This is also the perfect time to say, "I'm excited!"

Your third exercise will help **you tap into your feminine energy**. Different women have different relationships to the word "feminine." When I use the word here, I don't mean to imply that you necessarily consider yourself a "feminine" person according to society's expectations. That piece of your identity is up to you. What I do mean when I say tapping into "feminine" energy is your ability to reach inward and find that sense of body power and the spark that accompanies it. I'm talking about the thing you channel when you're feeling confident, sexy, and comfortable in your own skin. That energy that makes you feel desirable—that's what you want to channel, no matter what kind of woman you are.

Tapping into your feminine energy is easy and fun. You can do it by gyrating your hips in a circle, kind of like hula-hooping. I know it may feel silly, but this motion gets you out of your head, which is where your decision-making (and overthinking!) lives, and into your body, where your sensual, body power exists. Place your hands on your hips or over your womb and *feel* into your sexual, feminine power. Say a positive affirmation, such as, "I'm sexy," "I'm desirable," or "I'm irresistible." Notice any resistance that comes up, whether you laugh or think, *This is stupid, I'm not doing it*. What comes up for you underneath that resistance? There may be some discomfort or fear around allowing yourself to be in this vulnerable, sexual state. Can you identify where that insecurity stems from? Embrace your feminine energy and your sensuality, rather than push it away. Get comfortable in your exquisite body. Allow yourself to push self-criticism (especially body-related criticism!) to the side for now. Don't feel that you need to resolve it. This isn't the time or place for that. Tapping into your feminine energy isn't about suddenly resolving every insecurity you have. It's about allowing yourself to ignore those insecurities for the time being and just giving yourself permission to feel good and to feel grounded in your physicality.

Don't Have a Plan

In a perfect world, every date would be a smooth experience where you instantly click. But in real life, first dates are rarely stress-free. They can be awkward or a little messy, and it can take some time to get on the same page—or to even figure out if there's a possibility of getting on the same page. You're often a bundle of nerves and mentally preoccupied, trying to read your date and understand what they like, want, and expect in a partner, all while trying to make a good impression. The problem with having high expectations for how a date will go—and who your date is—is that it sets you up for disappointment. Unfortunately, the world doesn't play by your rules, no matter how much you want it to. When you have an expected outcome or agenda that's not met, it can cause you to be more critical and closed off to the experience. Disappointment happens when your expectations are not met, and that can lead to cynical dating energy. Not everything will go your way. Not everyone will be who you want them to be. In fact, most people won't be! But even expecting a bad date is expecting a certain outcome. If you can train yourself to not expect anything from a stranger, then you won't be horribly disappointed—and you may even be pleasantly surprised.

Remember, too, that every potential partner enters the date with their own set of experiences and expectations, which will differ from yours. The most generous thing you can do—and the best thing you can do for a positive outcome—is to acknowledge this to yourself ahead of time, and allow yourself to feel the date out honestly, rather than projecting what you want it to be, or trying to steer it in a certain direction. When you do those things, you're not really engaging with the person honestly, and you're not participating in reality so much as your own vision of how things *could* or *should* be. Try letting the situation be what it is—even if it's awkward or not what you'd imagined—and let the person you're meeting be who they are. Let yourself watch how things unfold and give yourself the opportunity to discover what makes this person tick. Who knows? Maybe there's no romantic chemistry, but you end up making a new friend. Or maybe you realize this person is perfect for your best friend, but not for you. Or maybe your date ends up introducing you later to your ideal match. If you allow reality in, rather than trying to fit someone or some situation into a specific mold that you had imagined beforehand, there may be possibilities beyond what you had conceived of.

When you value and respect yourself, you anticipate being treated a certain way. I'm all about getting the love you desire and not settling for poor treatment. However, you can't expect someone to know exactly what you want and how you want to be treated, and for them to behave in ways that are acceptable to you all of the time. One would hope that your date would be kind, courteous, and well-intentioned, but you're not entitled to these things. If someone treats you in a manner you consider disrespectful, you have every right to get up and leave. (And if someone makes you feel unsafe, please always *do* leave.) In general, though, try to keep in mind that someone may simply have a different set of expectations from you. Yes, there are social norms, such as arriving on time for a date, but not everyone operates from the same rule book. This may look like expecting your date to pay for the meal when they're expecting to split it, someone trying to kiss you on the first date when you don't kiss until date three, or the cutie from your date last night waiting multiple days to follow up when you're expecting a text the next day. If you're not on the same page, you can say something so expectations are made clear or you can decide to wait it out a little and see how their behavior unfolds as you get to know them better (unless they are crossing a boundary—in which case, always speak up). If you decide to communicate about it, make sure you frame things in a positive way, so the person understands that you are interested in them, rather than merely criticizing them. For instance, my client Megan was texting with a guy she matched with online before their first date. It turns out they went to high school together and he secretly had a huge crush on her. He was coming on strong by repeatedly saying how obsessed he was with her in high school and how beautiful he thought she was, and already calling her terms of endearment, like "baby love"—all before they met. This was a huge turnoff for her, but she was trying to keep an open mind. Their date went better than expected, but she was still frustrated by his enthusiasm, so she sent him a text the following day after he had already followed up saying, "I know it's a teenage dream come true ;) but can you turn down the hype just a bit? We're off to a good start and I want to make sure there's enough real-life substance to get so excited about. Maybe hold off on the pet names until we find some that are special to us?"

If you want more frequent or consistent communication and someone isn't being responsive to your attempts, be direct and say, "Hey, it makes me so happy to hear from you because communication between dates is how I feel connected and gauge your interest. If you want to continue seeing me, then I need you to be in touch more regularly." Then pay attention to what their actions are telling you. Being direct about what you want and need is important, but it's equally important to check in with yourself about how reasonable your request is relative to the amount of time you've been seeing that person. If you send this text after one date, you'll probably come off as too intense or needy. Many women tend to want a lot of momentum up front and want things to move quickly emotionally. While this is a completely natural instinct, and nothing to be ashamed about—especially when you really like someone—it's also good to question your sense of urgency and make sure you're not rushing things for no good reason. Rushing things along is usually a clear indication that your anxious attachment style is being activated and allowing these insecurities to rule your dating decisions can sabotage the start of a potentially great relationship.

Decide to Relinquish Control

Sometimes we subconsciously try to control other people, the situation, or the pace at which the relationship moves. We do this especially when we let anxiety or insecurity take over because we feel vulnerable and don't want to be disappointed or get hurt. Yet, part of a successful dating life involves stepping into the unknown and relinquishing control. Even if you're attracted to each other and they have the qualities you're searching for, there are factors outside of your control, like what *they* are looking for, and whether it's a good time for them to be in a relationship. At the end of the day, all you can control is yourself. You can control your actions and reactions, you can control the way you communicate and the way you treat someone, but you can't control other people or force them to date you. In fact, you should never have to convince someone to love you or want to be with you. I promise it will never turn out to be satisfying. So give yourself permission to let go, step faithfully into uncertainty, get comfortable living in the in-between, trust things have a way of working out, and ride the dating wave.

Look Like You/Be One of a Kind

You know who you are and what you're looking for, so the question is, does your outward appearance reflect this? Your personal style makes a statement to others about who you are and even what you value. This includes your choices in clothing, jewelry, accessories, hairstyle, and makeup or lack thereof. Whether you like it or not, people make automatic judgments and decisions about you based on these things. There's so much that's out of your control, so when it comes to conveying who you are through your appearance, delight in the fact that this is one realm where you can control something. Whether you're preppy in pearls and a polo, or a goth girl in black with facial piercings, it's all good as long as your outward choices align with who you feel you are internally. Are you proud of the image you're projecting? Does it say something about what you like or how you view the world? What do your choices say about your values and preferences to someone encountering you for the first time? Think about this carefully. Clue your date into who you are by the way you physically present yourself to the world. On the third date with my husband, I remember that he complimented my earrings and told me that he liked my wardrobe because it wasn't "cookie cutter." This compliment was so meaningful because I personally put a lot of thought and effort into how my outfits speak to who I am. So I appreciated that he not only noticed, but also seemed to really *see* me.

Now that we've discussed the importance of looking like YOU, let's explore what studies say about the most effective date outfits. I want you to be true to yourself, and at the same time, I'm here to provide you with guidance. If the following advice is helpful without leading you to discard your own personality or sense of style, then feel free to use this info.

In 2015, a British T-shirt company conducted a survey online asking 1,000 participants to match colors with associated personality traits and found that 56 percent of the respondents chose black as the top choice for many positive qualities, including intelligence, confidence, and sexiness. There's a reason why an LBD (little black dress!) is so popular. If you go this route, make sure to accessorize it to match your personality. Another good date outfit option is red, which was favored by men as a color they found attractive on the opposite sex, and women also chose it as the color that makes them feel sexy. In a 2008 study published in the *Journal of Personality and Social Psychology*, researchers found that "red, relative to other achromatic and chromatic colors, leads men to view women as more attractive and more sexually desirable" but "does not influence women's perceptions of the attractiveness of other women, nor men's perceptions of women's overall likeability, kindness, or intelligence." This means wearing a red dress may help boost sexual chemistry, but you'll still have to bring your stellar personality to the date if you want them to see you as more than just a hookup. Of course, take this color research with a grain of salt—if you love leopard print, rock it. And if you're not into men, maybe red isn't for you. Always take into consideration your hair color, eye color, skin tone, and pick something that makes you feel like a million bucks. I can't say it enough: Pick something that makes you feel like you.

If you're struggling to feel confident about your outfit selection, choose your favorite body part and select clothing that highlights it. If you love your long legs, wear a mini skirt or tight skinny jeans. If you have defined shoulders or a nice collar bone, try a tank or cold shoulder top. Emphasize the thinnest part of your waist with a wrap dress. Try a V-neck if you like your chest or cleavage. Toss on a pair of heels to show off your calves. Choose a bold lipstick to make your smile pop. There are so many ways to do yourself up in a way that highlights the thing you'd most like to show off. You can also play around with different fabrics that have their own associations, such as leather or lace. All this said, make sure you're not trying so hard for a look that you need to be constantly adjusting your clothing on the date or that you're secretly really uncomfortable in the whole time. All of this will give off a self-conscious vibe, which is the opposite of what you want. Your goal should be to feel comfortable in your own skin, and in your outfit. Please note: This doesn't mean wear yoga pants to a cocktail bar! Be emotionally intelligent about what's appropriate for the context, and make the best first impression possible. This doesn't mean you need to look like everyone else in the room, and it doesn't mean you need to dress to the nines every time you go out. Be aware of the world around you, but also give yourself permission to wear your hair how you like it—and don't be afraid to flaunt a little flair.

ON THE DATE

Though everyone is unique and has their own preferences, we know that the majority of women want certain things on a first date, thanks to the annual Singles in America survey conducted by Match. The survey polls over 5,000 U.S. singles between the ages of 18 and 70-plus every year, and most recently it has found that most women on a first date want the following: a compliment on her appearance (94 percent), her date to insist on paying (91 percent), to be waiting for her when she arrives (90 percent), a hug hello (82 percent), and a kiss on the cheek (71 percent). The most important way women want to feel on a date is comfortable (79 percent). We also know what women *don't* want in a date: checking your phone (90 percent), being more than fifteen minutes late (90 percent), having more than two drinks (81 percent), and ordering food for us (68 percent). Are these too much to ask? I think not! Though we can't control our date's behavior, we can control our own. Let's review some tips on how to be your best self so that you can sparkle and stand out from all of the rest.

Behave and Speak with Confidence

Simply put, self-confidence is mesmerizing and magnetic. We are drawn to people who know who they are and are unapologetically themselves. (In fact, research has shown that when you're confident, you're automatically perceived as more competent, even when you're not providing accurate information!) So, say things like you mean them. It's true that no one is confident all of the time, and we all have things we're insecure about or don't like about ourselves. Yet, your job is to lead with what you like and love, so save the self-deprecating remarks and practice self-compassion. You're the expert on yourself; no one knows you better, so speak with self-assuredness. Confidence means expressing your opinion, speaking your mind, or sharing about yourself in an honest and positive way. Being confident is *not* the same as being cocky or arrogant, which is a turnoff. Walking this line with grace is key since arrogance and cockiness usually backfire as they can reflect underlying insecurity that's covered up with this brazen, obnoxious attitude. For example, mentioning that you recently received an award for an accomplishment is not the same as bragging that you were better than everyone else or boasting how you deserved to be recognized.

What prevents us from feeling confident and comfortable in our skin? Usually it's shame about something in our lives. We hide our shame, insecurities, and hurts, and let them fester in secret, which only exacerbates those feelings. The problem with this is that creating a romantic connection requires authenticity and vulnerability, allowing someone to truly see you. Are you walking around trying to be perfect and not allowing others to see your tender parts? You might be hiding behind perfectionism, thinking it's protecting you, but really it's armor keeping others out. In her book *The Gifts of Imperfection,* Brené Brown says it best: "Perfectionism is not the same thing as striving to be your best. Perfectionism is the belief that if we live perfect, look perfect, and act perfect, we can minimize or avoid the pain of blame, judgment, and shame. It's a shield. It's a twenty-ton shield that we lug around thinking it will protect us when, in fact, it's the thing that's really preventing us from flight." It can be confusing to know how to present as both vulnerable *and* confident on a first date, so it's helpful to reframe vulnerability from a weakness into a strength. Maybe you go on a date while between jobs, despite feeling insecure that you'll be judged as unsuccessful. Being vulnerable means being honest that you're unemployed, but then sharing excitedly about how your time off has given you the opportunity to explore new options and passions. Maybe you live with your parents and feel insecure about that. Being vulnerable means talking about your living situation, while exuding confidence that it's allowing you to plan the next chapter of your life, or being proud that you can save up money to buy your dream house. Painting an un-ideal situation in a positive light isn't lying. This is actually how you should ideally see these situations, anyway. And talking about them out loud—admitting that you're a work in progress, but that being a work in progress is fun and exciting—will make you come off as much more appealing than if you seem to be pitying yourself for not having everything figured out or pretending that everything is perfect when it's not the life you want to be living.

Choose to show up confident in yourself as you are today, even if the circumstances of your life aren't exactly what you want them to be. When you allow your date to see you as you are, rather than the perfect version you'd like to present, you can create the authentic connection and relationship you've always desired since you're not pretending to be anything else.

Here are some ways to show that you're confident on a date. First, greet your date with a decisive hug or a kiss on the cheek, which is more intimate and less businesslike than a handshake. It's also usually a better way to start things off than with an awkward bobbing-of-your-head hello, or an embarrassing half hug or high five when you don't know what they were leaning in to do. I usually kick things off with "I'm a hugger" and open my arms. If you're not cool with physical touch, that's fine, just initiate whatever type of greeting makes you feel comfortable. You're looking for a significant other, so you want to see if there's a romantic connection. During your conversation, assert and stand by your opinions and beliefs, rather than say something you think your date wants to hear. If you don't agree with what your date says, respectfully share your stance. A friendly debate can be a fun way to banter and connect over ideas— especially between people who value intellect over other qualities. If you hate reality TV and they're going on and on about *The Bachelor*, you don't have to pretend to be into it to get them to like you. If they want to order a bottle of wine, and you're not a big drinker, say so. If you're a people-pleaser, curb that behavior by making yourself known. (Alternatively, if you tend to be more opinionated and aggressive, try to listen more and present your ideas in a gentler way than usual.) With that said, part of the beautiful thing about a partnership is finding someone who expands your world-views and ultimately causes you to grow and expand your identity. A common mistake I see people make is looking for someone who has all of the same perspectives, beliefs, hobbies, and backgrounds. Yes, you want to share some core values and life goals, but *you don't want to date your clone.* Assume you have things to learn and new perspectives to consider. Embrace differences—they are interesting.

Ultimately, you can show off your confidence by being decisive, but not inflexible. For instance, when choosing a restaurant, provide a few options or compromise on the location. Tell your date what looks good on the menu, but don't insist they try something that they really don't want to. Tell your date you want to do an activity rather than another meal, but then don't veto all of their suggestions. Express your preferences, but don't be demanding.

Assuming you're comfortable with physical touch, take and create opportunities to test the chemistry and show that you're warm and affectionate. If you feel confident that your date is romantically attracted to you, toward the end of the date you can touch their shoulder when you laugh, lean into them when they say something sweet, or grab their hand when you walk alongside each other. If they're reciprocating or creating their own opportunities for touch outside of the initial greeting or casual hug goodbye, then it's a good sign they're into you, too. To play it safe you can always mirror their level and type of contact. On a first date, touch should be light and infrequent, otherwise it may turn into more of a hookup situation. Pulling or leaning away is typically a sign that someone does not want to be touched, so read their reaction and if you see that, don't touch them again. Of course, if you don't like physical affection or advances so early on and prefer not to be touched, speak up—always respectfully. If that's the case, just make sure you communicate down the road once you're ready for more affection since they can't read your mind.

Fake It Till You Make It

We don't always feel confident and worthy of love and admiration, especially after a bad date or being rejected by someone we're really excited about. We're usually our harshest critics, and sometimes we need a day or two to wallow in our own self-loathing. You're not going to feel happy, energetic, and optimistic all of the time, and that's okay. That said, when you're meeting people and looking to make a romantic connection, you can't be a total Debbie Downer. Think about how you would feel if your date was super negative the whole time! That doesn't mean you need to be a glass-half-full kind of person if that's not who you naturally are, or hide your snarky sense of humor, or change your personality. Dating confidence is all about owning who you are, and projecting this positively in your interactions with others. On a scale from one to ten, where 1 = you cancel last-minute because you're insecure that your date won't like you and 10 = you're rock solid in who you are and ready to show up in all of your glory, where does your dating confidence fall? If it's under a five, it's time you *fake it till you make it*. This approach is actually backed by science.

The psychology behind fake it till you make it is that your actions can lead to feeling a certain way, rather than waiting to feel a certain way to take action. Change your behaviors and trust that the feelings will follow. For instance, as

I mentioned earlier, when you fake a smile, research shows it creates feelings of happiness and decreases depression. Psychologists at the University of Kansas had participants hold chopsticks in their mouths to physically create certain facial expressions, and a mimicked smile even resulted in a lowered heart rate and less stress. Psychologist and professor Richard Wiseman's "As If" principle proves that "we are what we act." Wiseman ran a speed dating study in which one group behaved normally with their date, while another group was instructed to pretend they were already in love, by doing things such as gazing into each other's eyes, touching hands, and whispering secrets. At the end, participants were asked to rate on a seven-point scale how close they felt to their date, and whether they'd like to see each other again. Those faking romantic interest rated their closeness one point higher on the scale, and 45 percent said they'd like to see their date again, compared to only 20 percent in the normal group. This study suggests that behaving like you're in love can lead to actual feelings of falling in love. So, if you pretend to be confident, such as making eye contact, breaking the physical touch barrier, or sharing something vulnerable about yourself without worrying how the other person will respond, you can trick yourself into really feeling confident. Eventually you won't need to pretend since you'll be motivated to naturally behave in ways that are consistent with your new identity.

What "Being Too Nice" Really Means

Have you ever heard the rumor that it's not good to be "too nice"? The truth is it's not really about whether or not you're nice. What this expression means when it comes to dating is that it's not good to be too accommodating. You need a backbone. You need to assert boundaries and stand by them. When you don't respect your own boundaries early on with someone you barely know, it signals that you don't respect and value yourself. When you bend over backward to please, you'll be taken advantage of, and it's not attractive. People want a partner, not someone they can dominate or constantly need to take care of (*Fifty Shades of Grey* is fiction!). Honor your own boundaries, and the right partner will, too. When you say you need to be home by a certain time, end the date. If you want to see your beau, ask them to come to you instead of always offering to drive to them. When they ask for a favor, ask for one back. Be an equal partner, command respect, don't put in all of the effort, and ask for what you want.

Be Interested/Be Interesting

Talking passionately about your hobbies, goals, and achievements shows that you enjoy who you are. You're awesome and have so much to be proud of, so make sure your date knows that you're the whole package. Excitedly sharing about yourself doesn't mean you're bragging, arrogant or egocentric, so you don't have to wait to be asked a question before providing information—just dive in. (That said, remember to gauge their reactions and ask them questions, as well. No one wants to talk to someone who *only* talks about themselves!) When I was dating, I found that I could instantly put people at ease striking up casual conversation as if I already knew this person without the stiff, formal salutations. It was usually a short funny story about something that happened to me that day. It eased both of our nerves and led to free-flowing conversation without any of the awkward initial interactions. So greet your date with a hug and tell them about your nutty Uber driver! Take initiative to make the first conversational move instead of waiting to be approached. It can be a simple, "Wow, I love the ambiance in this restaurant, good pick! Have you been here before?" which compliments their taste and can lead to a discussion about what local restaurants you each like. You could also say, "Oh good, I'm so relieved you look like your profile photos; this date is automatically off to a great start," which can lead to a funny (and unfortunate!) story about a time you were catfished. It's helpful to have some canned go-to date stories that have been tested. Since you'll be going on many first dates, you'll have a lot of similar conversations, which means you'll get tons of practice telling the same stories, refining them, and picking ones which are a hit. Humorous stories about things you've done or have happened to you always go over well.

When you're confident in yourself, you have nothing to prove, so it means you can also sit back and ask questions, rather than dominate the conversation with your entire life story. Creating a give-and-take will ensure that you're a fantastic conversationalist. Plan on listening more than you speak, but don't be afraid to interject your own story or comment if questions aren't asked in return—just don't steamroll your date. Rather than ones that elicit a one-word response, ask open-ended questions; for example, "How did that make you feel?" "Tell me more about that," "What do you think about XYZ?" Express genuine interest in who your date is and what motivates them. The best impression is made when you're present and attuned. Stephen Covey, author of *The 7 Habits of Highly Effective People*, writes, "Most people do not listen with the intent to understand; they listen with the intent to reply." Stop trying to think of your own response or comment while your date is talking, get out of your head, and give that person all of your mental presence. Since this type of focus is rare these days, you'll likely make an impression. Do your best not to make any snap judgments about whether or not you want to see the person again. There'll be plenty of time to reflect after the date ends, so just be in the moment. This should go without saying, but no texting or social media scrolling while on your date. Your phone, smartwatch, and any other gizmos should remain out of sight.

Take the opportunity to learn about your date and uncover what matters to them. Digging deeper is refreshing and welcomed by others who are also dating with intent and looking for a relationship. In fact, researchers at the University of Arizona found that a happy social life is related to having less superficial small talk, and more substantial, deep conversation. In the famous 36-question experiment, Arthur Aron and colleagues had participants ask each other increasingly intimate questions (such as, "For what in your life do you feel most grateful?" "What is your most treasured memory?" "If you could change anything about the way you were raised, what would it be?") and found that personal disclosure impacts closeness and attraction. The study even led to two participants getting married. Also, in support of mutual self-disclosure and vulnerability, the Singles in America survey found that 80 percent of singles welcomed talking about religion, money, and politics on a date. This may make you uncomfortable, but all of this research indicates that to create meaningful connection, you need to be talking about what matters. The key here is diving deeper into what matters most to you, so ask the questions related to your core values and don't be reticent to inquire about these "taboo" topics, which really aren't taboo.

You can start off with a general exploration of your date's lifestyle and experiences, with questions such as: "What does a typical weekend look like for you?" "What's your dream vacation?" "What do you love most about your job?" "What's your greatest accomplishment?" "What are your favorite ways to unwind?" "What's one ability you wish you had?" "Why do you love or hate social media?" "What's your most embarrassing moment?" Then ask follow-up questions based on what they share. I highly encourage you to ask additional core value questions so that you can discover any commonalities, learn about your differences, and uncover any potential deal breakers. This isn't an interview, so instead of asking question after question, allow it to take a more natural course by sharing your own answers and organically steering the conversation toward the topics you'd like to explore. For instance, if you're politically inclined, talk about something you saw on CNN that day and ask your date if they have an opinion. If you're close with your family, tell them about something fun you recently did with your siblings and then ask about their family. If you just adopted a dog, ask your date if they've ever rescued a pet or grew up with animals. If you love nature and the outdoors, tell them about a hike you took last weekend or the vegetable garden you planted and see if they share any similar hobbies.

At the end of the day, what we remember most about people is how they make us feel, so help your date feel good and put them at ease. Allow them to shine. Look for ways to make them feel special and offer up meaningful compliments based on things you learn about them, their idiosyncrasies, and mannerisms. Don't forget to compliment their appearance too, which, according to the Singles in America survey, 90 percent of singles agree is an impressive first date behavior. Be confident, be an excellent conversationalist, and talk about what matters. Your date will be impressed and dying to see you again.

Leave Them Wanting More

A little mystery is a good thing. That doesn't mean playing games, it just means not trying to cram everything about you into one date. Offer yourself up in bite-size pieces so that your date has time to digest all of your amazingness. Allow intimacy to build and develop with time spent together. According to Match's survey, two and a half hours is the sweet spot for length of a first date; any longer and your chances of seeing this person again start to decrease. If you're a chronic over-sharer, you may want to take this duration seriously and aim for a hard stop. Otherwise, if you're really jiving with someone, and the feeling is mutual, ride it out and go for a natural end point. The point is, give this lucky guy or gal a reason to look forward to learning more about you on a future date. One of the best feelings is walking away from a captivating date with the sensation that you've known this person forever. It's not that you know everything about them, but it's how they make you feel—alive, understood, connected, and comfortable.

Truth be told, I had a six-hour first date with my husband, so I myself didn't adhere to that two-and-a-half-hour guideline! Conversation flowed so smoothly and we just kept talking. He texted the next day to ask me out again, so sometimes a long first date works out. If the date is going splendidly, trust your gut about what feels right, but otherwise it's best to leave them wanting more. Know your own tendencies and figure out what's best for your style of communication and pace of getting to know someone. Once you know yourself and you've applied boundaries, you'll know when to make the exception. Similarly, a client of mine named Alexandra was connected to her date, Lauren, through a mutual friend. They met up for lunch, which led to a walk, which led to coffee, which led to cooking dinner together. And now they're about to celebrate their tenth wedding anniversary and just had a baby. Alexandra told me she'd never had a date like this before, but because she'd practiced having boundaries in the past, she knew that this date was different.

We all have pasts and complicated histories, but don't bring all the drama to a first date, otherwise you'll be red-flagged. Be open, but don't unpack all of your emotional baggage on the table. For instance, if someone asks why you're single or what happened in your past relationship, don't complain about your ex or give a play-by-play relationship history. Instead, share from a positive perspective your love lessons about what you now know you need in a partnership, what you learned about yourself, and future romantic goals. With time, you can open up more and share the hurt or not-so-pleasant parts, but do this once they've earned your trust. Being vulnerable means being open to love despite being hurt and disappointed in the past, but it doesn't mean having verbal diarrhea on a first date.

TO KISS OR NOT TO KISS

Did you know that there are trends in people's preferences about whether or not they like to kiss on a first date, according to their gender? Locking lips is more important to women than men when determining whether a partner is a suitable fit. Researchers at Albright College found that women placed more emphasis on kissing when assessing a mate, and as a way to initiate, maintain, and monitor a relationship with a long-term partner. Men, on the other hand, placed less importance on kissing with short-term partners, and used kissing to increase their likelihood of having sex. From an evolutionary perspective, women have evolved to make snap judgments based on the quality of a kiss, almost like a sniff test, since we are the ones at risk of getting pregnant and want to make sure we're passing on strong genes. If you've ever had a bad kiss—too much saliva, teeth bumping, bad breath—you know what a turnoff it can be.

Here's what we know about kissing on a date. The Singles in America survey found that 44 percent think a first date kiss is inappropriate, which means the majority would be down for a smooch. Half of men and women think *only* kissing is appropriate after a good first date, so save fooling around for later. We also know 95 percent of single men are extremely in favor of women initiating a first kiss, so if you're feeling it, go for it. In LGBTQ relationships, 57 percent of singles expect a kiss, 25 percent expect to make out, and only 30 percent expect no physical affection at all. At the end of the day, you'll have to make your own call based on what you want and the signals you're receiving from your date.

And sometimes signals can get crossed. You may think you're giving off a "not interested" vibe, but they're not picking up what you're putting down. For example, 74 percent of women offer to pay a bill because they don't want to feel obligated for anything else, such as a kiss or second date. Yet, 71 percent of men find it attractive when women offer to split the check. He might assume you're just being polite and not get the hint that this is your way of communicating that you're not feeling it.

To avoid any awkward or #metoo moments, think about what you want *before* you get to that moment in the date. What are you feeling? What does your gut say? If you're not ready for a kiss but still interested, you can say, "I don't kiss on a first date, but I'm looking forward to it when I'm more comfortable" to make it known you're not rejecting them, but that you need time to warm up. If you're definitely not interested now or ever, it's always best to be assertive and straightforward: "I'm flattered and this was fun, but I'm not interested in moving this forward." (Read the next step for other ways to cut things off gracefully.) If you're hoping for more, but unsure if your date is receptive, you can be patient and see if they initiate, or you can be up-front and ask whether they'd like a kiss, since consent is always cool. If you're not feeling that bold, when in doubt, play it safe with a hug or kiss on the cheek. Sometimes this can turn into more. For instance, a lingering hug with a slight pull away and eye contact tends to set the scene for a kiss on the lips. A kiss on the cheek may elicit an "I was hoping for the lips" response from your date, in which case, go in for the kill.

KEY TAKEAWAYS

Self-compassion, vulnerability, and confidence are all you need to make an incredible impression on a first date. So, own your personality and be true to you. Here are your key takeaways from step 4:

♥ To prepare for your date, turn your anxiety into excitement and get in touch with your sensual energy.

♥ Keep an open mind and communicate about what you need.

♥ You can control yourself, how you communicate, and how you treat someone, but you can't control other people, the pace of the relationship, or force someone to like you.

♥ Make sure your personal style reflects who you are on the inside and boosts your confidence.

♥ To project confidence, greet your date with a warm embrace, assert your opinions and preferences, and be decisive but not inflexible.

♥ Don't be too accommodating, and respect your boundaries.

♥ Take the initiative to start the conversation with your date, and make sure to create a give and take by asking many open-ended questions that explore their core values and what matters most to them.

♥ Leave your date wanting to learn more about you, rather than disclosing your entire life story on a first encounter.

♥ The majority of singles are down for a first-date kiss, and men are wildly in favor of you initiating one, but when in doubt, ask your date if they're comfortable locking lips, or wait it out and let them initiate.

Step

5

WHAT TO DO AFTER THE FIRST DATE

YOU ARE THE DRIVER, not the passenger, of your dating life. You get to decide if you want to see someone again or not. You're in control of managing your expectations. You can date from a secure attachment style, rather than riding the roller coaster of the anxious-avoidant trap. All of this empowered dating behavior sounds good, right? Let's dive into how to make this a reality.

DECIDE WHETHER YOU WANT
TO SEE THE PERSON AGAIN

Other dating books will tell you to wait and see if he calls, as if you're supposed to sit around passively twiddling your thumbs, giving away all of your decision-making power. The wait-and-see approach also assumes you definitely want to see this person again, as if you'd be so lucky to have them pick you for another date. *Screw that.* This book is all about what *you* want and empowering *you* to pick. I will say that there is a way to use silence and patience as an empowering strategy, which can be challenging if your anxious attachment style is activated. If you can gauge interest, there is power and confidence in being the one who is pursued. Yes, you can be the one to ask a man out, to follow up, to take action, but you can also relax and make time and communication between dates work to your advantage. This comes from a secure mind-set. Allow him to come to you, and in the meantime spend some time thinking about whether or not you even want to go on another date, and if so, why? Since you're dating with intent, your answer better include a response that's more than "because they're insanely good-looking!" Be honest with yourself about whether they seem like a promising partner. Are you overlooking red flags, or ignoring deal breakers because you're super attracted to them? If you do want to date hot people just for fun, by all means do it—there's no shame in it—but you don't need the strategies in this book for that, which is why we are focusing on dating with the goal of finding a partner. Based on what you learned on your first date, is what you know and like about them enough to warrant a second date? Ruling someone out is part of the dating process and reflects that you're being purposeful and proactive in your choices about what's best for you, regardless of whether your date wants to see you again. Many women get too focused on whether they were chosen for a second date instead of deciding whether *they* want to choose to see that person again. If this is a one-and-done date, don't feel bad if you're leaning toward no. No one wants to date someone who's not into them, so being honest with them is the kind thing to do if you're just not feeling it. And what if they don't want to see *you* again? It's okay! Not everyone is going to be for you. You do not need validation from every person you go on a date with. You are looking for someone who is completely taken by you and can't wait to spend more time with you. Once you've gotten clear about whether or not you want to move forward, there are several courses of action you will need to take.

If You Don't Want to See Them Again

You chatted or texted to plan your first date, you've gotten together once, or maybe you've gone on multiple dates, but you realize that you're no longer interested. How do you handle breaking it off before you're even official? Do you:

A. Ghost them (just straight up stop replying)

B. Slowly fade away and hope they get the hint

C. Make *them* dump *you* by acting like a jerk until they realize they're no longer interested

D. Tell them clearly but kindly that you're no longer interested

If you guessed D, you're correct! There are so many nuances in dating and in entering into a relationship these days, that calling it quits before it ever really takes off can be a confusing situation. I'm not a fan of one-size-fits-all rules, but if someone expresses interest in seeing you again, I do think you owe them a response. Sometimes there's an innocent disconnect, where one person thinks it's a great date, while the other doesn't. If they pursue you for another date, you must clearly communicate that you don't want to move forward. I'm a firm believer that the best course of action is to be transparent and straightforward. It's always courteous to not waste someone's mental energy wondering if they'll hear from you again. I'm sure you'd appreciate being treated in the same regard. Wouldn't it be refreshing if we knew each other's intentions and didn't have to second-guess everything? That's what dating from a secure attachment style is all about—communicating your desires, even if it means letting someone down. Strive to be kind when doing this. Wrap things up neatly with a bow so there's no lingering confusion about where you stand. Within twenty-four to forty-eight hours after the date, send a concise text: "It was really nice meeting you last night, but I got more of a friend vibe. Good luck out there!" or "Thanks so much for dinner. Unfortunately I didn't feel a connection, but I appreciated our conversation. Take care."

Here's some other dating etiquette on calling it quits. First and foremost, if someone sends you an online message and you're not interested off the bat, no need to respond at all or engage in conversation. If your convo has fallen flat and fizzled, unmatch and move on. If you've been chatting online, texting, or had a phone call with someone who's trying to meet in person and you decide they're not for you, say something along the lines of, "Thanks for the chat, but I don't see this going any further." If you've made firm plans, always cancel rather than no-showing: "I know we have plans, but

I've had a change of heart and don't think we'd be a match. I'm sorry for any scheduling inconvenience." (You can read more about breaking it off with someone you've been out on multiple dates with in step 6.)

If You Do Want to See Them Again

Here's the deal, when a man is into you, he'll be happy to hear from you, so if you're inclined to send a follow-up text about having an awesome time, or pass along a funny meme or interesting article about something you discussed on the date, go for it. This behavior won't push him into *not* liking you. Match's survey found that 94 percent of men are pleased when a woman is the first to call after a good first date, so being proactive is welcomed. The caveat here is that "good" is subjective. You may have been smitten, and super attracted to him, while he was lukewarm. Or maybe he put you in the hookup bucket, which is why he still did things like try to make out or take you home but doesn't want to pursue you further. You can look at someone's body language, aura, and energy on a date, but you may be too eager and misinterpret or read into some of these signs. We've all been in that confusing situation where you say goodnight and they say, "This was fun, we should do it again sometime," but then you don't hear a peep. As we discussed earlier, you should also be taking this time to really think about whether *you* want that second date, or if you just want to be wanted by someone. Is the challenge of making him want you so appealing that you're not being honest with yourself? Take time to reflect.

So how do you figure out if they're into you after just one encounter? The only way to really tell how someone is feeling is when their actions match up with their words. On the date, if they're telling you that they're having a great time, being affectionate, or even suggesting something you should do together on a future rendezvous, but don't offer up a firm date or time, then only time will tell if they follow up and follow through.

(Now is a good time for me to mention that while this book is intended for everyone, some of the advice in this section is going to skew more toward heterosexual trends because we have more data about those types of relationships. Hopefully in time that will change.)

When someone is on the fence about you, being the one to initiate can actually be a turnoff, or it likely won't sway him in a positive direction. It's kind of like how guys don't want to ask for directions; they're wired to be stubborn and figure it out for themselves. Of course that's not all men and this is a stereotype, but in general, he needs to decide for himself that he wants a second date. He should want to go out with you again because he was blown away by the incredible human being that you are, *not* because you have to push him or gently remind him that you exist. Real talk: He hasn't forgotten about you; he just wasn't that into it. You'll know he's not gung ho because you won't get a response, or you'll be "benched" and put in his rotation, mostly for casual hookups, and not because he wants to court you and bring you home to Mom. Basically, he'll give you just enough attention to keep you on his radar, but it's rare that this will develop into a relationship. It's one of the most frustrating places to be stuck in your dating life.

I know that's not what a modern day, go-getter woman wants to hear, but that's been my personal and professional experience. A man in his masculine energy wants to take action, pursue, and dictate the rhythm of communication. If he's impressed on the first date, he'll naturally initiate and want to see you again—no subtle coercing or forcing necessary. It will feel easy. The truth is that it's unlikely that your witty, perfectly crafted text that you spent hours debating whether or not to send (and which your best friend weighed in on) will be the thing that causes him to want to take you on a second date. Being in your feminine, receiving energy, means allowing him to put in the effort to prove he's worth your energy. Be responsive to his efforts by communicating, suggesting, and complimenting, which are green light signals that you're also interested and won't reject another date. But don't put in all of the work. If you're the one to suggest getting together again, let him balance your ask by planning the date. Mirror back someone's level of effort and energy. Cute follow-up conversation should be light and entertaining, such as a beautiful photo from the hike you're on, or asking for a song recommendation. This is like a light tap on the shoulder. However, messaging them a very long text or asking too many questions about the details of their day may be seen as too intense this early on. It could be perceived as an interrogation that can feel like too much pressure to respond to. If their effort and energy is not enough for you, rather than trying to force it, let them go; they're not the right fit. Remove the pressure of feeling like you have to be in charge, stop stressing, and kick back with confidence that you're desirable and worth being pursued.

I know I talked mostly about heterosexual dynamics here, but this isn't so much about gender roles—rather it's about trusting that if there's chemistry, connection, and you're both emotionally available, a next date will happen, regardless of who initiates. Flow with it, take action when you feel inspired and confident, and not because you're insecure or your attachment system is activated. Don't stress too much about it because if they're jazzed about you, and you're jazzed about them, there will be a second date, and it doesn't matter who initiates.

WHAT TO DO WHEN YOU'RE REALLY EXCITED ABOUT SOMEONE

When you're really into someone, first manage your mind-set. It's easy to jump ahead and start envisioning your wedding, so reel it in. A lot of clients tell me, "But I never get excited about anyone," so they instantly put this potential partner on a pedestal, forget about their deal breakers, and are willing to tolerate subpar behavior because of that spark. Pace yourself. Being treated well, respected, and communicated with consistently should be a minimum requirement to entering into a multi-date relationship with someone. This is your ground-level standard. These are not meant to be outstanding characteristics; they are meeting an entry-level threshold. You will not go out with someone unless these criteria are met. This reflects your self-worth.

A smart dating strategy is to date multiple people at once so that you're not putting all of your eggs in one basket. That way, you won't go overboard too early with one person, or be too disappointed if it doesn't work out since you'll have options and distractions. I know—this may feel unnatural at first, but it's actually a smart strategy. Some find it too exhausting or hard to keep track of who they're telling what to, some don't like the idea of someone they're dating having intimate emotional exchanges with multiple people at once, and others can't stand the thought of kissing or being physically intimate with more than one partner at a time. Despite all this, there are several reasons it is a smart strategy. First, when you're excited about someone, it becomes easy to rush into things and scare that person off, not to mention getting your hopes up and feeling let down when it doesn't work out. Second, most men date multiple people at once, so you are putting yourself on an equal playing field (if you date men!). I highly encourage you to continue to go out with new people, especially after one great first date. If anything, it will help put into perspective how much you truly like someone, and give you lots of practice so you'll be well seasoned by the time you meet a keeper.

Oftentimes we equate the feeling of being excited with chemistry. You want fireworks. In fact, you won't even consider a second date with someone if you don't feel that instant pull and magnetism. Yes, ultimately, if you can't develop the sexual attraction, the relationship is a no-go. However, the key word here is *develop*. It's a common misperception that there's either a spark or there's not, but attraction can actually grow with time. This is especially true for women, who from an evolutionary perspective value partners who are socially dominant. This means our level of interest can increase when someone possesses qualities such as being well-liked and respected in their community, a provider of a certain lifestyle, and of course someone who makes us laugh, even if they don't look like a movie star. If someone has the core values and qualities that you've prioritized, be patient and see if love will grow as you go on more dates and build emotional intimacy, and even a foundation of friendship.

Even if you do have chemistry with someone right off the bat, this spark can dupe you into believing there's a stronger connection than what actually exists. It's easy to be fooled by an intense physical attraction. That's because from a neurochemical perspective, our hormones, such as dopamine, oxytocin, serotonin, noradrenaline, vasopressin, estrogen, and testosterone create the sensation of lust, which is what that honeymoon phase is all about. When you interact with your crush, your brain releases these feel-good chemicals that create a euphoric, infatuated, and excited feeling. The "cuddle hormone," oxytocin, released during physical contact like hugging and sex, creates feelings of attachment. We know from neuropsychological research that your amygdala, the portion of your brain responsible for making judgments and rational decisions, basically takes a nap while in this smitten state, and you can easily miss red flags or compromise on deal breakers. You're blinded by love—well, lust. Don't mistake this love potion as true compatibility. When singles ask me how long to wait before having sex, I always bring up this neuroscience because sex can confuse things since it's unclear whether you're feeling connected due to the hormones, or because you truly like who this person is at their core. Dig deep to explore who they are and whether they have the qualities and values you desire *before* hopping in the sack. When you feel the spark, enjoy it, but take things slowly enough that you can see with clear eyes who you're engaging with. If you are dating with intent to make a lasting connection, make sure you're staying true to your defined values and deal breakers.

Get Clear on Why You Like Them

Let's say you go out with someone and you know that you definitely want to go on a second date with them. Ask yourself why. What excites you about this person? Be cautious of falling for someone because they *make you feel* a certain way, such as less lonely, more interesting, or desired. Yes, how this person makes you feel will influence how you feel about them, but I want you to choose to go on a second date because you like who *they* are. This is something people get tripped up on all the time.

A first date is just an introduction to someone, and you're not going to know everything about them from a brief interaction. But when you're dating with intent, your goal is to take advantage of that time together to have in-depth discussions about what matters most to each of you. Reflect on what you learned and ask yourself if you like enough about who the other person is—not how you feel around them—to go on a next date and explore more.

On the other hand, it's easy to get overanalytical and pick someone apart—we humans love to focus on the negative. Instead, focus on what you enjoyed and think about whether there might be more there. So often men are focused on green lights, and women on red flags. Stop looking for what's wrong with someone and identify things that lead you to believe you'd be a strong match. The only instance when you should focus on the negatives is if they have any deal breakers based on your core values. A second date is simply a commitment to learn more about someone; it's not accepting a marriage proposal. Is the potential you see with this person worth another couple hours of your time? If so, go out again and enjoy yourself.

Practice Patience AKA Remember That You Have a Life

As we've discussed (and as you probably know all too well!), when you're really excited about someone, you may have the tendency to rush into something or prioritize this person more than you should. This might look like canceling all your other dates, deleting your dating profile, or clearing your schedule so that you're available for a second date. Don't do any of these things. Remember that you have a life. You're not exclusively dating this person, you've only had one date, and your world should absolutely not revolve around when they might call or want to see you again. If they call when you're at the gym, finish your workout before calling back. If they ask you out for next Saturday night, but you're already going dancing with your girlfriends, keep your plans. Tell them that you're busy that night and suggest a different night when you are free. If you're watching your favorite TV show, finish the episode before responding to their text. Remember that you are priority number one, so don't make someone else a priority until they prove to you that they're worth it. You have a big, passionate, fulfilling life that you need to keep living. Plus, keeping yourself busy will help you keep your giant crush in check so that you don't go gaga too quickly.

Let the relationship take a natural course. There are no rules about how long you should wait between dates before seeing each other again. It should be a comfortable pace for both of you, and of course what works with your schedule without rearranging it for someone you barely know. If you wait too long, however, the initial excitement may fizzle, or both of you could meet someone else who you prefer to pursue, so aim to go on a second date ideally within another week of the first date. I went on a first date with my husband on a Thursday, then we had a day-date two days later on Saturday, which went so well that we decided to meet up later that evening after we each wrapped up plans with other friends. When the attraction and excitement is mutual, roll with it.

DATE SECURE

One pattern I've noticed and even experienced myself is that if you have an anxious attachment style, you may accidentally rule out a secure person too early because you're not used to being pursued and communicated with clearly. You're accustomed to chasing and the intense push-and-pull that typically comes with dating an avoidant. You've associated this intense dynamic with thinking you really like someone, when in actuality, it's just your activated attachment system.

When dating a securely attached partner, you may accidentally misattribute your initial disinterest to a lack of chemistry. You may think they feel too safe or boring, since you're used to anxiously waiting by your phone for a text and unsure if your date wants to see you again. You might even engage in some avoidant behaviors yourself, like ghosting or causing drama, like pushing them away so that you then have to work hard to get their attention again. I know, it's twisted! Be weary of friend-zoning a secure person too early. There's a good chance there could be a solid foundation and the fireworks display is just delayed. You have to get out of your own anxious way and realize that in the past you've mistakenly associated the angst at the start of a relationship with love, when really it's only your activated attachment system. You basically have a distorted love meter. You think that if you're pretty, funny, or smart enough, they'll finally like you back. If you put out or are good enough in bed, they'll want to date you or give you the attention you're craving. If you're patient, understanding, and stroke their ego enough, they'll finally give you the commitment you desire. The thing is, you are already enough. When you date from a secure mind-set, you'll see

dating isn't about proving yourself. You'll lose your taste
for this type of game playing and stop chasing. You'll find
someone who will willingly fill your love tank without
having to work for it, just by being you.

You'll know you're playing into the anxious-avoidant
trap if you're constantly trying to get someone to like you,
when you don't even know *why* you like them. This is more
about seeking validation and playing into insecurities than
about choosing a partner from a confident, secure mind-set
and believing you have the power to pick them, too. With
that said, it's your job to take responsibility for your anxious or avoidant patterns. Activated anxious behaviors
include texting or calling a bunch of times in a row when
you're upset or insecure, feeling untrusting and jealous,
threatening to leave or breakup with no real intention to
do so, or giving your partner the silent treatment in hopes
they'll come crawling to you. Avoidant behaviors include
being overly picky about small things you don't like and
using these as an excuse to keep your partner at a distance,
belittling or criticizing them, shutting down or ignoring
them when they come to you with relationship concerns,
and withholding physical and emotional intimacy when
they're seeking closeness.

As you get closer to a partner and establish a relationship,
which can be tricky to do when you pair an anxious with an
avoidant, do your best to communicate about your fears and
behaviors to your partner so that they can better understand
you and not let unhealthy dynamics spoil your relationship.
As a former anxiously attached gal myself, dating a securely
attached partner has significantly helped ease me into more
secure ways of interacting and behaving. I've been cheated
on in the past, and was in a long-term relationship with an

avoidant, so I'm hypersensitive to perceived "threats." One of my triggers is shady phone behavior. I'm very aware of when my old attachment style is triggered, so I take the responsibility to tell my husband what's going on, and together we work through it. Since he loves me and gets me, he takes the time to make sure I feel good about any concerns or insecurities that flare up, rather than getting angry or making me feel crazy. For instance, one late night I noticed him glancing at his phone and it brought back memories of my ex secretly texting someone inappropriately. I immediately felt flooded with feelings of jealousy and asked him what he was doing. He said that he was checking his fantasy basketball stats, and I admitted to him I was triggered and had a surge of fear that he was talking to girls online. He offered to show me his phone and then jokingly asked if my anxious attachment style wanted a hug. I instantly felt soothed and secure. This is the type of communication that can help heal your old wounds and strengthen your relationship.

When you practice dating from a secure mind-set, and your date also has a secure attachment style, it should feel easy and you'll know where someone stands. You can model a secure attachment in your dating life by affirming that dating is an enjoyable process, where you can have fun meeting new people and seeing where things go. Realize that you have the power to pick your partner, too. Trust that you're a catch who deserves love and intimacy, and refuse to settle for scraps of someone. If they won't give you the commitment you desire, walk away because you know there are *many* other worthy candidates. Believe that a relationship worth pursing must have safety, trust, consistency, dependability, and open communication. As an anxious, learn to articulate your insecurities and fears to your partner. Ask directly for what you need, rather than acting out negatively in an attempt to reestablish connection—this typically just pushes someone farther away. Avoid jumping to conclusions and catastrophizing as much as possible. When you're feeling triggered, use healthy and soothing coping skills to calm down before talking to your partner. Try to trust that someone who is right for you will make an effort to understand you and step up to meet your needs rather than make you feel even more invalidated and insecure. As an avoidant, realize you can find ways to maintain independence, even when giving to your partner in a committed relationship. Realize that depending on someone does not make you weak, and vulnerability is actually a sign of emotional strength. Commit to turning toward your partner for closeness and conflict resolution, even when it feels easier to ignore their "neediness." Put in effort to operate from a teammate mentality to create a sense of healthy interdependence.

KEY TAKEAWAYS

You should leave this step clear on *why* you want a second date and empowered to choose, rather than waiting around to be picked. You now have the strategy to either call it off or move forward with a potential partner, all while dating from a securely attached mind-set. Here are your step 5 takeaways:

💜 You'll know someone's interested when their actions match up with their words and they follow through.

💜 If you're both jazzed about each other, then a next date will happen, regardless of who initiates.

💜 Take action when you're inspired and confident, and not because your attachment system is activated.

💜 When you're excited about someone, don't put them on a pedestal and forget about your deal breakers.

💜 If someone has the majority of what you're searching for, give it time to see if a spark ignites.

💜 Don't mistake intense physical chemistry for a strong underlying connection.

💜 Don't put your life on hold for someone; prioritize yourself until they prove they're worthy of your time.

💜 Be cautious of friend-zoning someone too quickly because you're used to the angst and intensity (i.e., your activated anxious system) of dating an avoidant.

💜 Date from a secure mind-set by minimizing anxious and avoidant dating behaviors.

Step

6

WHAT TO DO ON DATES TWO TO FIVE AND BEYOND

YOU HAD a successful first date and want to see where this connection could be heading. In the past you may have struggled to navigate the gray area of an undefined relationship. This is where many people psych themselves out or self-sabotage. Not anymore. In this chapter, we'll talk about the best ways to confidently and securely nurture a connection, and let things develop so that you can decide if the person you've met is a keeper.

SHOW YOURSELF

As I said at the very beginning of this book, vulnerability and authenticity are your sexiest qualities. When you feel secure about who you are and don't feel the need to pretend anything, you can finally create a true connection with someone else. Show up in all of your genuine splendor. Have confidence, even when you're still working on yourself. You will always be a work in progress. Love doesn't happen when you've reached some sort of end point, it happens *while* you're investing in yourself. Close your eyes for a moment, take a deep breath, and affirm, "I am enough."

Honestly, it sounds trite, but the commonly offered advice to "just be yourself" is applicable when it comes to your love life. Romantic connection grows by sharing the real, raw, and not-so-perfect parts of you with someone else. This is how we let people truly see us. Usually the things that make you feel vulnerable are the things that create connection when shared. Why do you think that producers on reality TV shows, such as *The Voice*, highlight something traumatic, intense, or transformational that happened to the contestants? It makes them instantly relatable, and it makes you want to cheer for them. We get to know others and feel a connection with them when we hear their backstories and what shaped them into who they are today.

Dates two through five are this exciting sweet spot when you get to give the person you're dating the opportunity to start to truly see you. Over the course of multiple dates, peel back your layers, whether it's about how your parents' divorce affected you, the time you were let go from your job and decided to start your own company, or a sports injury that forced you to take on new hobbies. Let someone in by sharing with them your defining moments. It's always best to be able to articulate what you've taken away from these experiences to show how you've grown. This highlights your resilience and makes you a desirable partner—someone strong that overcomes challenges. If you're still working through a difficult time, that's okay, too—you don't have to have life all figured out. Baggage stops being baggage when you've taken the time to thoughtfully process how you've grown from painful experiences. Just be careful to not unpack all of your baggage in one sitting. Reveal yourself layer by layer with each date, and pay close attention to your partner's response. Are they supportive? Do they make you feel accepted, or judged? If you sense that the person isn't ready to go that deep yet or isn't being present and engaged, adjust how much information you're sharing and how quickly. Think critically about the signals you get from that person; after all, there is a big difference between someone who needs a little time to become emotionally intimate and someone who is only half-listening because they don't really care to get to know you on a deep level. When you lower your defenses and allow someone to see this authentic, imperfect version, it's important that you feel understood and seen. Make sure you're seeing what's beneath their surface, too. If you and your date seem to be on the same page and you want to tell them about your life, allow yourself this vulnerability.

COMMUNICATION BETWEEN DATES

When you're excited about someone, you may have the urge to talk to them all the time. This is a great feeling, and a completely natural one. That said, now is the time to be thoughtful about the frequency of your communication and the content of it. Pace yourself. Let your crush miss you a little bit! Contacting someone you're newly dating too much can come off needy and smothering—even if you don't intend it to be that way at all. This especially goes for texting 24/7 when you're in the getting-to-know-you phase. If you find yourself unable to stop texting the person—or you're just thinking about texting them constantly—this might be an indication that you have an anxious attachment style which is being triggered. No matter the case, practice a secure mind-set. Use texting for logistics to set up a next date or some flirty banter here and there, but do your best to save meaningful and vulnerable conversations for in person, where you can make eye contact, read each other's facial expressions, and see how they respond to what you're sharing. Those are the moments that truly create intimacy and connection, so don't cheat yourself of those incredible experiences. A real relationship cannot be created through your phone. If the person texts you about something that's better suited for a face-to-face convo, you can be friendly but honest by saying something like, "I'd love to tell you about it on our next date" or "That's a story better suited for in person!" Gradually increase the frequency and amount of conversation the longer you're in each other's lives. And get comfortable picking up the phone to hear their voice, rather than always texting, which can build a false sense of intimacy.

GETTING PHYSICAL

The desire for physical intimacy is extremely unique to each person and each couple, so there's no scientific answer as to how the timing of physical intimacy affects relationship success. Have there been couples who date and even get married after sleeping together on the first date? Absolutely. Do I recommend it if you're in search of a serious, committed relationship? No. Here's why: It's not a value judgment on my part—its more about the psychology of the thing. Sleeping together backfires when it leaves little to be desired or discovered about the other person. People tend to value what they have to work hard to get. My opinion is that sexual intimacy should enhance the bond you're already building. There's a commonly held belief that you should wait until date three to sleep together. This is totally arbitrary and there's nothing magical about date number three. What's more important is that you feel safe, which usually comes with developing emotional intimacy. For some, this happens after one date, for others it takes multiple weeks or months. I generally recommend waiting until you know whether you like someone enough that you want to continue seeing them, you feel confident they'll want to continue seeing you after you have sex, and you're both ready to see if the chemistry you've been feeling translates to the bedroom. Let yourself look forward to sex—there's no rush. In the meantime, enjoy steamy make outs and other sexual or sensual acts as you feel comfortable.

Studies have shown, however, that a foundation of friendship leads to a more satisfying sexual relationship. Psychologist Laura VanderDrift and her colleagues at Purdue University performed a study where they asked participants what they valued most about their relationship. The study found that those who answered "companionship" and "friendship" also had the highest sexual satisfaction in their relationships. This suggests that a healthy connection outside of the bedroom often leads to a healthy one inside of it. A relationship built solely on sex will burn out with time. Don't forget about the powerful love potion of neurochemicals that can make you feel infatuated and attached. All of the smart dating strategies you've been implementing will allow you to create a solid foundation first so that physical intimacy will increase your bond, rather than mask a false one.

Sexual compatibility *does* matter in a romantic relationship. Otherwise it's just a friendship. You're looking for a BFF *and* a lover, right? People vary on their level of desire and preferred sexual frequency. Some view it as a very primal act, void of emotion, and others use it as a primary way to feel emotionally connected. Some love to experiment with positions, role-play, and sex toys; others like it straight up missionary. Whatever floats your boat! There's no right or wrong here, but it's about what works for you *and* your partner. I often work with couples who come to therapy because of a mismatched sex life, with one partner desiring it much more frequently than the other, or one person craving a more adventurous sex life. Sexual compatibility isn't necessarily something you just "find" in a partner; it can be cultivated, developed, built together, and improved. However, if your sexual preferences are tied to your core values, pay attention to this. If your conflicting desires are just too different (or make one person really uncomfortable), be honest about it. No one should have to compromise on what's most important to them or put themselves in a situation that feels physically or psychologically unsafe. Better to explore and discuss this early on (I'm talking about in the first few months, NOT the first few dates!) than invest too much time.

Being True to Yourself About When You're Ready

From the get-go, a sexual energy between you and your partner is important for being *more* than friends, but that doesn't mean you have to do anything outside of your comfort zone. You can be flirtatious in your smile, eye contact, the way you touch their arm, or in making sexual comments and jokes, but none of these things involve rounding the bases.

An empowered woman decides when *she* wants to get physical. So often I hear of women taking it further than they're comfortable with because they want to please their partner or think it will get them the commitment they want. Respect yourself and your boundaries. Set the standards for how you want to be treated. **Physical intimacy with you is a privilege, not a right**. The right partner will be patient and go at a pace that you set. Do what feels right for you, be aware of the reasons why you want to be sexually intimate with this person, and move at a pace that makes you feel secure.

When and How to Talk About It

Sex shouldn't be something you're on the fence about. From a safety standpoint, it's best to talk about sex before you're in the moment and feeling the feels. It's a good precaution to explicitly ask, "Do you have protection?" and "When was the last time you were tested?" so you can be prepared for safe sex and any STD disclosures. The reality is that many consenting adults don't talk about sex in advance, but sex can dramatically change the dynamic of the relationship and unearth any covert expectations, such as monogamy. You should never assume because someone is sleeping with you that they're not also sleeping with other people. If this bothers you, it's best to talk about sex and your expectations prior to sleeping together. If you are concerned about avoiding awkwardness, the key is making sure the topic of sex gets woven into the conversation organically. You can broach the topic in a lighthearted way, such as commenting on a sex scene in a movie you're watching together or by asking your date about their favorite positions (if it makes sense in the moment). However sex comes up, it can then naturally lead to talking about your own future bedroom adventures. If you're a straightforward gal, by all means bring it up point-blank.

Sex is a two-way street, and your partner's sexual needs are also important. You may be ready, but they may not. If you're mature enough to be having sex, you should be emotionally mature enough to talk about it. Learning about your partner's timeline doesn't mean there's any pressure to appease them and meet it. It just means having a conversation about each of your preferences or expectations. This requires you to assert your boundaries, such as, "I only sleep with someone when I'm in an exclusive relationship" or "Sex is really important to me, so I like to test it out before committing to someone."

Sex is something you want to feel good about. No one likes that icky, regretful feeling afterward, like it was just another notch on their belt, or the angst that comes with wondering whether this person will still want to see you again. If you are truly dating for keeps, make sure you feel secure and confident in the relationship before becoming sexually intimate. When you've taken time to ensure this person has the qualities and values you desire, and you're ready for that step, then go for it and relish the sexual side of things!

I also want to highlight that there's no shame in sleeping together early on if that is what feels right. There's a myth that "purity" is valuable, and women are routinely shamed in this culture for enjoying sex and pursuing pleasure when they should not be. There's absolutely nothing wrong with being in touch with your sexual side. Celebrate your body, own your pleasure, and banish any absurd ideas that women are more valuable if they've had sex with fewer people. This double standard and the Madonna-whore complex are misogynistic facets of our culture that thankfully are fading away with time. You are beautiful, strong, sexy, and should never feel shame about pursuing happiness and being honest about what you want physically.

Consent

Let's be honest. Talking about sex before you do it doesn't always happen. Sometimes you're caught up in the moment, it feels awkward, or you don't want to "ruin the mood." Taking control of your dating life means taking control of what happens in the bedroom. This does not mean you need to have a long emotional talk about what sex means to you. But there is one thing you must do: Get comfortable giving consent and get comfortable saying no. We can't expect someone to read our minds and just magically know what we want or what feels good—or conversely what we do not want and what does not feel good. To be a good sexual partner, it is essential that you participate in giving consent—or not—as you see fit. Reduce confusion and hesitation by giving clear sexual consent: Verbally say "yes" or "I want this." It is not enough to avoid saying no. It's unfair to yourself and it is unfair to your partner if you are unclear. It is especially important to be extra clear if you are under the influence of drugs and alcohol—and even then, many people argue that consent can't truly be given. Keep in mind that giving consent for one sexual act, like a passionate make out or oral sex, does not automatically give consent for another act—like penetrative sex. Each new step or activity requires a new verbalization of consent. And you have the right to change your mind at any time.

HOW TO KNOW WHEN TO COMMIT

Remember when I told you that when my husband and I met, we went on multiple dates in the course of one week? Well despite my strong feelings for him, I was still openly going on dates with other men. And when he first asked me to be his girlfriend, I actually said no because I wasn't ready to be exclusive. I was recently single, enjoying dating around, and wanted to be intentional about picking my best match. I only wanted to commit to someone that I knew had the qualities I was hoping to find in a husband, which meant taking my time to evaluate potential partners, and being purposeful in my dating decisions. I communicated honestly that I wasn't ready for the title of girlfriend and asked him to be patient with me because I could see building a strong foundation with him. We continued to date and communicate openly about our feelings so that we could manage expectations and get on the same page—and look where it led!

Since this is your dating life, *you* decide when you want to take the next step. If someone tells you that they only date one person at a time, don't feel pressured to preemptively cancel your other dates and convert to their dating style. Simply let them know that you prefer to date casually until you're ready to commit. They can then choose whether they want to continue seeing you, and if not, there's an abundance of other people who do. If the person you're dating isn't ready to commit, it's important that they are still being present with you and engaged in developing your relationship. I know it may be uncomfortable thinking that they are dating people other days of the week, but focus on your time together and letting them really get to know you. You're not in competition with the other women, so it's not about proving yourself or trying to be the most fun.

Dating Red Flags

End the relationship if you experience the following red flags:

»→ They date other people but expect you to be committed

»→ They only send late night booty texts ("u up?") and don't take you on any formal dates

»→ They check in constantly about who you're with and they behave possessively

»→ They actively have an addiction and are not seeking treatment

»→ They make no effort or care to impress your friends

»→ They dodge or ignore all of your questions about what they're looking for

»→ They pressure you to do sexual acts outside of your comfort zone and/or try to convince you not to use protection

»→ They are verbally, emotionally, or physically abusive

Creating the foundation for a great relationship means giving your partner the time and space to choose you, too. Try your best to be open-minded by allowing this to happen. You'll know you're being taken advantage of if they no longer seem to be putting in effort to learn more about you, or you're just "hanging out" instead of going on dates. The relationship should still feel like it's progressing forward, even if they are seeing other people.

Eventually, if you think that your core values are aligned, and you feel in your gut that this relationship has potential, you'll want to test it out by putting both feet and fingers in (no more swiping online!) to commit. That's because relationships require effort in order to succeed. When your attention is elsewhere, it's impossible to give your budding relationship the nurturing it needs to blossom.

Read the Signs

You should experience a few things with your potential partner before committing.

1. You're most excited to spend time with this one person, and you're starting to prefer their company to going on first dates with new people. This is often the first sign. If you're casually dating around, this person feels like your home base—the person you want to talk to before falling asleep at night. The important reflection point here is to make sure it's not just a case of feeling comfortable because you've spent a certain amount of time together, or that it feels less scary than new dates. Instead, it's that you feel like your time is better spent—or would be more enjoyable—than with other people you're seeing, and that it eclipses the excitement of meeting new people. You should enjoy your time together, and the person should make you feel special, seen, and adored.

2. They've proven consistency. They've put in consistent effort to court you and haven't resorted to "Netflix and chill" for every date. Consistency is also important in

terms of their demeanor and personality. Sure, people have good days and bad days, but you should have a good sense of the person's emotional range. For instance, you've seen them stressed out more than once and were glad to see that they consistently had a good outlet for their stress, rather than taking it out on you. Look, also, for consistency in behaviors. It's a bad sign if they love bomb you with grand gestures one day, only to treat you like sh*t the next. Make sure they don't play games and give you mixed signals, and that their words consistently match their actions and intentions.

3. You continue to see promising behaviors, traits, and core values that you desire in your ideal match, without the presence of deal breakers. You should already have a picture of the lifestyle you currently live and the future you desire, who you are, and your major goals. Between dates two and five, you are exploring those things in your potential partner. Remember not to be too rigid and to allow yourself to be surprised and delighted by someone else. They may have different passions from you, which can work well if they're flexible on the things that are most important to you. That way, both of your needs are being met without compromising and violating what matters most. The more you get to know about them, the more you like and admire them.

4. You've been able to communicate through conflicts, disagreements, or disappointments. All couples have conflict—fighting and bickering is normal, but there's a healthy way go about it, and being able to disagree without deeply hurting the other person, as well as being able to repair the rift after those arguments is key. If you can't

communicate in a healthy way, your relationship won't work. Period. Do you feel like you can voice your opinions or concerns and still be respected, listened to, and conversed with calmly? Or do you fear that this person may mock you, dismiss your opinions, roll their eyes, or say something mean-spirited when they disagree? In the times you've had fights, are they nasty, throw down, blow out arguments? Or are they more like debates, where both people are being respectful on a basic level even in a heated disagreement? Couples researcher John Gottman found four communication patterns that reliably predict the end of a relationship. The following are what Gottman calls the four horsemen of the apocalypse: criticism, which is blaming a relationship problem on your partner's perceived personality flaws; contempt, which is acting from a place of superiority and disgust with your partner; defensiveness, which includes denying any responsibility for the problems, acting like an innocent victim, or counter-attacking your partner while ignoring his or her complaints; and stonewalling, which is shutting down completely and refusing to offer any verbal or nonverbal responses to your partner's attempts at communication. If you witness any of these behaviors, especially early on, you're likely in for a bumpy ride, so I urge you to address the communication issues ASAP, or get out.

When you can say yes to these four points, it's time to give it a real shot. Stop shopping around, and don't succumb to the "grass is greener" dating mentality, where people get stuck thinking that something even better could be around the corner, and never end up committing to anyone. That best thing may be right in front of you, and the worst thing you can do is pass over it without giving it the attention and effort it deserves. You can always break up with someone if it's not working, but you may not be given a second chance, so commit and see. When I decided I was ready, my husband and I became exclusive a couple months into dating, two months later we became boyfriend and girlfriend, and within a few more months we grew in love (I'm not saying "fell" because it was an intentional process), and then moved in together. It was clear that he was my person. We got engaged on the anniversary of our first date and married less than a year later. Your epic love story is out there, too; start writing it!

Have the Talk

How do you actually have a DTR (define the relationship) convo?

Let's quickly clarify the reasons you *don't* have a DTR talk: because you're anxious about a nebulous relationship status; because you desperately want a partner and don't care who it is as long as you're not alone; or because you think giving it an official title will cause the avoidant person you're dating to change their behaviors. You should commit because *you're confident* in what you've already developed, not the other way around. When you feel secure and are dating someone who is just as excited about you, a DTR talk will come naturally and be a welcomed discussion since you're both validating that you're ready to dive in and take the next step.

Every relationship will move at its own unique pace. There's no magic rule or number of dates by which you should be having a DTR talk. If you need a guideline, I'd say between those initial two to five get-to-know-you dates it's appropriate to ask this person what they are looking for; that way you're not investing too much time in someone who isn't looking for anything serious. If they said that they're just looking for something casual and fun, then that's what they mean. Believe them and don't overanalyze it or stick around because you hope they'll change their mind after spending time with you. If you're both open to the idea of a relationship, then continue dating so that you can figure out if you want that relationship to be with each other.

When you're dating someone with a secure or anxious style who's into you, your partner will be enthusiastic about locking it down as an exclusive partnership earlier rather than later, and there won't be a lot of second-guessing or waffling. When you're dating an avoidant, however, they will likely dodge your questions, or give you a confusing or ambivalent response—like "Let's just see where this goes" or "Why do we have to put a label on it?" Again, there's no one-size-fits-all advice for when you're both ready to enter into a relationship. One couple could see each other multiple days per week for hours at a time and communicate frequently between dates, while another could only go on a date once per week for multiple months, so it's less about the length of time you've been in each other's lives and more about how you're feeling. If you need another general guideline to keep you moving forward, I suggest checking in with yourself around date ten as to whether you feel ready to enter into an exclusive, committed relationship. An exclusive relationship means you're seeing each other monogamously. Though nuanced, there is a difference between an exclusive relationship and using the titles of boyfriend or girlfriend. An exclusive relationship is kind of like trying it on for size to make sure the relationship is still heading in a positive direction. Once you've tested it out for a few weeks or a couple of months, an official title can come with its own ask or declaration.

Of course, a DTR discussion requires vulnerability since there's always the potential that you will experience rejection or hear that they're not ready to date you exclusively, but vulnerability is what creates true connection and intimacy. Your new narrative is a mental script of hope, abundance, and affirmation that you're worthy of reciprocal, committed love. Let that script prime you to behave confidently in line with your desires. If you're ready for exclusivity, the title of "girlfriend" or something similarly significant, then take action to explore where your partner is emotionally, and do your best to be open-minded and sensitive to what you find there. If you're in a heterosexual relationship, give your man some time and space to bring up this type of discussion on his own. It will likely thrill him to take the lead and initiate, and he's probably already given you signs, such as planning special dates based on your interests, asking to meet your friends, and making future plans, or he's made comments to suggest how much he's enjoying getting to know you and told you that he's excited to see where this relationship will go. If you're unsure, a securely attached dater will state how they feel without guaranteed reciprocation; for example, "I really like you and don't want to see anyone else. I'm deleting my dating profile. How do you feel about that?" or "I'm really enjoying our time together and think I'm ready to give this a real shot. How do you feel about only seeing each other?" You can also toss out an open-ended question, such as, "How do you think our relationship is going?" or "What does the next step in dating each other look like to you?" If you receive an unclear response, ask for clarification: "I'm not sure that

I understand what you want. How do you see us moving forward?" If they need more time, or there's no clear path forward, it's up to you whether you want to stick around and see what develops. It's one thing if your partner asks to go at a slower pace but is still eager to continue the courtship. If this is the case, they will still be planning dates with you, having emotionally intimate conversations, and making you feel like a priority. However, I caution you from investing too much energy that's not being returned with the same effort. Do they seem checked out? Has it become more of a sexual relationship? Do you rarely get a prime-time Saturday night date? I've seen too many women play it cool, hoping that if they are "chill" enough and wait around long enough they will finally get the commitment they desire, when in reality they are being taken advantage of. When you chase and invest too long or too much in someone who is not reciprocating, you'll wind up feeling resentful and unappreciated. Honor your emotional needs. If you desire a relationship with this specific person, and you've spent enough time together that you're sure you're not rushing it, don't settle for a half-in, half-out situation. With that said, I also want to highlight that society sometimes makes us feel a sense of urgency about locking someone down or starting a family by a certain age. This internal struggle can cause you to rush things along, and the problem with that is that it usually scares people off. There's a delicate balance between being empowered, honest, and self-expressed versus consumed with emotion, excitement, and anxiety, which causes you to move faster than is necessary. At the end of the day, you deserve a partner who is just as open and willing as you are. If ultimately you decide that they're unable to meet your needs, tell them that you can't continue to invest if you don't want the same things. Then, walk away from the relationship, and be proud that you asserted yourself and did everything within your control.

CALLING IT QUITS

Between three to five dates, you've likely learned quite a bit about someone, probably shared some romantic kisses (if not more), and established emotional intimacy. You've brought up what you're looking for in a partner, or at least your intentions to form a relationship with the right person. If you realize that this relationship isn't what you want after all, there are ways to be kind but direct about how you feel. If it's still early on, you can text, "Hey, I've been thinking a lot about you and our conversations. I want to respect both of our time and energy and be transparent that at this point I don't think we're the best fit/want the same things. I really enjoyed getting to know you, but we should end things here."

Any time you can communicate on a phone call or in person, the better, since it significantly humanizes the experience and seems more personal and considerate. If you've decided in advance that you want to end it, pick up the phone to let them know you had a change of heart and spare them the time and excitement of getting ready for the next date, thinking they have plans that night, and then blindsiding them.

My rule of thumb about texting versus calling versus in person is that before five dates, texting is okay; after five dates, you need to call them to have a conversation; and any time you're exclusively dating someone, an in-person breakup is warranted. Focus on how *you* feel, and how your values or visions for the future don't align. Try not to be critical of *the person* or to point out their flaws. The goal is to explain why *the connection* between the two of you isn't strong enough. At this point, your partner may have questions about what went wrong, so you can shed some light on why you're calling it off. Be generous and allow the person you're breaking up with to ask questions. If you've been in their shoes before, you know how confusing an out-of-the-blue breakup can be, so this is their chance to gain closure. Allow it to feel like a conversation, rather than a one-sided cutoff, while still sticking to your guns and not letting yourself to be talked out of your viewpoint. Sometimes it can be hard to put your finger on what's missing, especially when someone is wonderful, so try your best to identify what feels off (keeping in mind that you don't want to be hurtful for no reason). And if you're not really sure why it feels off, it's okay to say that. For instance, "I know myself and how it feels when it's right. It's difficult to articulate, but I should be more excited about the potential for this relationship than I am after spending this much time together." Remember that this is *your* dating life, so do what you feel in your heart and gut is right. If your partner becomes defensive or tries to convince you otherwise, don't feel the need to justify your decision; you know what you want. Stay calm, stay firm, stay kind.

In the past, any number of things may have led you astray—old dysfunctional narratives, insecurities, activated attachment systems, or unrealistic expectations. Those may have made it difficult to trust your own judgment. Now that you've done some self-work, check in with yourself to see if anything is being triggered before ruling out a quality, secure catch. If nothing is being triggered, trust yourself and move on to the next person!

KEY TAKEAWAYS

You can create true connection through authenticity, vulnerability, and believing that you're enough, with nothing to prove to your date. As you peel back each other's layers, keep in mind the following takeaways from step 6:

💜 The frequency of your between-date communication should increase the longer you're in each other's lives, but always save meaningful conversation for in person.

💜 Physical intimacy should strengthen the bond you've built, occur when you're ready, and always come with consent.

💜 The best practice is to talk about sex before you have it, and never assume exclusivity just because you're sleeping with someone.

💜 Eventually you need to commit to dating one person so that you can nurture a budding relationship enough for it to blossom.

💜 Before committing, make sure you prefer to spend your time with this person over other dates, there's consistency in your partner's behaviors, their actions align with their words, there aren't any known deal breakers, and you can successfully communicate through disagreements.

💜 A securely attached dater will have a DTR talk when the time is right, so express your feelings and your desire to take it to the next level, and don't be afraid to walk away if your needs aren't being met.

💜 If you don't want to see someone again, be transparent and straightforward that you're no longer interested in moving things forward, and kindly provide as much closure as you can.

Step

7

HOW TO PICK YOURSELF UP IF IT DOESN'T WORK OUT

THERE ARE only two directions a relationship can go: be together forever or breakup—no pressure! Nobody has a crystal ball that tells you when you'll meet your keeper, so it's about dating new people until you do. Unfortunately, not every rejection is so easy to get over, and sometimes a big breakup can be soul-crushing. It can feel like losing your emotional home and mourning the loss of the future you envisioned. Despite that pain, spending too much time chasing after your ex or trying to fix a broken relationship keeps you stuck. For this reason, it's valuable and healthy to know when to call it quits or how to move on when you didn't see the end coming. Let's explore how to cope, heal, and start over without emotional baggage so that you can reopen your heart to bigger, better love.

FEEL YOUR FEELINGS

As a species, we thrive and survive in close, intimate relationships. A romantic rejection leaves us feeling unprotected, alone, and like we don't matter. When you suffer a romantic loss, you may feel like a zombie, walking through a world that has recently collapsed. This may not be what you want to hear, but the best way to get through your uncomfortable emotions is to face them and actually sit with them. Experience these painful feelings. Stop intellectualizing, and be with yourself on an emotional level.

I advise clients to do the following exercise: Close your eyes, put one hand over your heart and the other on top of your stomach, take some deep breaths, and then see what emotions bubble up inside of you. You may think you know what you're feeling but be surprised at what you find when you sit in silence. It may be rage, remorse, loneliness, devastation, stress, embarrassment, betrayal, shame, or an array of other conflicting emotions, like relief and joy. A brain imaging study performed by psychologists at UCLA shows that when you become mindful of your emotions and able to identify them, your brain activates the region associated with emotional regulation. This means that by assessing and correctly categorizing what you feel, you are taking the first step to gaining control over that feeling. In contrast, when you don't carve out time to process and label your emotions, your brain doesn't regulate the response you're having, and as a result, you may experience those emotions more intensely. So observe your emotions judgment-free, without labeling them as good or bad. Trust that there's a stable part of you that can hold strong, which will allow these feelings to flow in and out like waves, knowing none of them will stay put for very long, and none of them will knock you over entirely, even if it feels that way. Rather than resist, welcome each emotion. It may feel silly, but speak to the emotions out loud: "Hello, anger. I see you, I feel you, I honor you." Then go about your day without doing anything rash to change it.

When You Choose to End It

Sometimes the person you're seeing breaks your heart. But sometimes you break your own heart. And that's okay. When it's not right, be courageous and end the relationship. An intuitive way to know that the relationship isn't right is when your head and heart are not in alignment. Maybe you can't put your finger on what's wrong or missing, but just the fact that you're torn between your head and heart is important information. When your heart is asking for more or believes more exists, honor that—even if you don't know what the alternative looks like. If your head is telling you it won't work because it's too complicated or you find yourself compromising too much or you're losing yourself in the relationship, believe your head. Not everyone has instant clarity that they've found their forever person. Relationships can improve with effort, but after you've invested the work and professional assistance, and you're still torn, listen. Sometimes you know the relationship isn't right because you find yourself constantly questioning it. Maybe you're always wondering if there's a better match out there, or your love tank still feels empty even when you've learned to speak each other's love languages, or you just feel like you make better friends than lovers. It might be time to walk away. (Reread the end of step 6 for how to break things off in the best way possible.) When you're with the right person, your head and heart will be in agreement. Believe that there's a kind of love out there that will make it clear why it didn't work out with anyone else.

When the Other Person Ends It

Hold on to your hat—you're about to go for a ride on the roller coaster of grief. There are common stages of breakup grief through which everyone will eventually pass. The key word here is *eventually*, since similar to grieving a death, there's no exact timeline, and everyone copes differently. You'll move through feelings of denial, during which you may be in shock that it's actually over or feel emotionally numb. This is like survival mode for your mind, when your brain and body are preparing for a big transition. As your new reality sinks in, you'll experience the stage of bargaining and anxiety, during which you may try to convince your partner to stay with you, making unrealistic promises in an attempt to salvage the relationship. You'll spend *a lot* of time ruminating and obsessing about what went wrong, and missing them. The problem is that the more time you waste begging for your ex back, the more you convince yourself that the only way to be happy is with them by your side. However, the one who broke you can't fix you. It's hard, but the best thing you can do is admit to yourself that the relationship was not perfect. If it had been, they would not have chosen to end it.

You'll also likely experience intermittent anger, which could be directed at your ex, yourself, the universe, or even your friends and family for not understanding your pain. Often the thing living underneath anger is a deep hurt. I would be remiss if I did not acknowledge that sometimes this sadness can spiral and can include emotional and physical symptoms. You may even feel hopeless about your future. It is normal to feel all of this for days or weeks (depending on how long or serious the relationship was), but if you find that it's going on for months, your sadness over the breakup may have transformed into a more serious depression. If you're struggling with depression, please seek professional help. In addition to this, do your best to take care of yourself by eating healthy food, getting enough sleep, being careful not to abuse substances, and especially by getting some exercise, even when you don't feel like it, since doing so releases endorphins and dopamine, which will actually make you feel a little better.

When you've been broken up with, some of your pain is probably coming from feeling blindsided, a fear of change, the distress of starting over, worrying how others will judge you, or feeling like a failure. The thing is, there are no failures in dating—there are only experiences from which to learn and grow. Think about that: There are no failures. Every relationship ends until you get to the one that doesn't—and you learn things about yourself from each of those relationships, which makes you more equipped for the next one. Your biggest transformation occurs from your lowest low, so even though you're hurting, the meaning you make out of your pain is gold. When you can make this positive reframe, you'll turn your setback into a comeback, and it will be fierce!

One day, you'll feel lighter, like the mental load of these emotions has been taken off your shoulders. You'll reach a place of acceptance, which is the final stage of grief. Some days, you may feel triggered and get sucked right back into the intense earlier stages; however, you'll find that you can more quickly and easily get to the calmer, more contented place of acceptance as time passes. In the acceptance stage, you've made peace with the end of the relationship, even if you aren't happy about how the breakup went down. You're optimistic about your love life and what the future could hold. You can get to a place of acceptance once you've forgiven yourself for things such as sticking around for too long or investing time, energy, and finances when it wasn't reciprocated; for continuing to pour love into a taker who didn't give back; for compromising on your core values, ignoring your intuition, lowering your standards, and not honoring yourself while in the relationship. Focus less on trying to grant forgiveness to your ex and ruminating on their behaviors, and more on being compassionate toward yourself for your own transgressions and loving the parts of you that feel shameful. The way to release ill will and resentment, and slowly reopen your heart, is by embracing love for yourself. Real forgiveness comes when you create space for it, and it takes time to get to that better place. Forgiving your ex doesn't mean you have to maintain or rebuild a friendship, or even communicate with them directly. In most cases, I recommend hard boundaries, like removing them from social media and no contact, especially at the beginning of the breakup. Eventually, you may get to a place where you can genuinely wish them peace from afar, realizing that people who cause you pain are likely in pain themselves. The reality is, a broken heart is painful and it takes time to recover, so be patient and kind to yourself.

NO REGRETS

When you've been rejected or your heart is broken into a million pieces, it's easy to act irrationally. You may not recognize yourself: sending nasty, hate-fueled e-mails; entering stalker mode driving by their house; creeping on social media to see who they're dating; drunk dialing and leaving voice mails you'll regret in the morning; double or triple texting when you don't hear back from them; or scheming ways to get revenge. I once had a client who dated a woman, and after they split, she called his place of employment and left ranting voice mails for all of the C-level executives about what an a$$hole he was—all because he didn't want to date her exclusively after they'd been sleeping together. Another client's ex-wife poured bleach all over his suits when they divorced. Do your best not to succumb to your worst instincts. These types of behaviors are not healthy. Though acting out may give you instant gratification, behaving with grace during rejection (admittedly easier said than done) will make you feel better in the long run and preserve your dignity. By behaving irrationally in the face of pain, you're not honoring yourself, and in fact you are probably confirming to the person that they made the right choice to let you go. Wouldn't you rather be the one that got away?

When you're hurting, try out the following healthy coping skills, which are backed by science to improve your mood and decrease symptoms of depression and anxiety:

»→ call a friend

»→ listen to music

»→ meditate

»→ exercise

»→ take a walk in nature

»→ color a mandala

»→ knit

»→ read a book

»→ watch something that makes you laugh (like a comedy skit or cat videos on YouTube)

A less scientific (but some would argue equally helpful) approach is to visit your stylist for some hair therapy since a new haircut and color literally changes your appearance from the person you were when in the relationship. This "breakover" will have you walking away feeling lighter, both physically and mentally.

If you're feeling alone, remember to lean on your friends who will give you a sense of belonging. Rather than ex-bashing, ask them to tell you about the ways they noticed you weren't your best self in this relationship. When you're blinded by love, it can be hard to really see the relationship for what it was, so your besties can bring a fresh perspective. You may be surprised to see how you didn't value yourself, or how you gave away your power when dating your ex. Or let them distract you with funny stories from their lives that have nothing to do with your ex. Let them be there for you.

HOW TO LET GO

It's easy to catch feelings when you're really into someone and get attached. It honestly doesn't matter whether it was one date, six months, or six years; when you've been rejected, that fixation can fester. It's important to ask yourself whether you were truly into them, or into the *idea* of them. Sometimes we get swept away by the thought of a person or the thought of being part of a couple. When someone shows up with all of your must-haves, it's natural for you to get really excited and miss signs that it might not actually be everything you want it to be. Or maybe they were everything you wanted, but if it didn't work out, something was off. It won't serve you to deny this. Take your ex off the pedestal and focus on what you wish you could change about them, why you don't make the best team together, or how your needs went unmet. Your ex might be a catch, just not *your* catch, so let them swim back into the dating sea.

It's also important to reflect on whether you truly liked yourself in this relationship. In what ways did it or did it not bring out the best in you? Did you tend to feel needy, jealous, insecure, crazy, or sad? Were you constantly trying to impress them or seek approval? Did you feel you could be relaxed, authentic, and vulnerable? Did you feel seen, and as though you were enough? Did you let your ex define how you felt about yourself? Even though you may not feel this way right now, the relationship ending was probably a blessing in disguise.

In order to let go, you must first understand that your pain is actually a physiological response to the withdrawal from love. Though it *feels* like you just lost the love of your life, the obsessive, can't-cut-the-emotional-cord sensation has to do with how your body is wired for connection, more so than whether or not the person was "The One." Our nervous system and brain chemistry can synchronize with our partner's in a phenomenon called interpersonal synchronization, in which individuals begin to physiologically mirror the people they're with. This allows us to share deep emotional states, such as empathy, fear, and even the stress hormone cortisol. A researcher at the Cognitive and Affective Neuroscience Lab at CU Boulder found that when holding hands, lovers' heart and breathing rates sync up, and it can even help reduce one partner's pain. So sometimes your connection is truly much more than emotional. In addition, studies have shown that breakups can affect us on a neuropsychological level similar to how our bodies process drug withdrawal. Dr. Helen Fisher and her colleagues did a study which showed that when in love, you're actually in an addicted state and dopamine is released in the reward center of your brain, giving you a hit of pleasure similar to the response it has when on drugs. When you go through a breakup, that daily "hit" of love is taken away, and your body is no longer getting "high" on your partner's affection and attention. This is why you miss them so intensely and crave contact with them, which is your body's way of urging you to get your next "fix." Research has even shown that a breakup activates the same brain region where our bodies process physical pain—rejection really does hurt. People with an anxious attachment style struggle the most with a breakup, since they worry more, have lower self-esteem, and tend to personalize the rejection as a reflection of their worth. They cling on longer and try harder to make it work, and they have a harder time self-soothing and regulating their emotions. No matter your attachment style, work to reframe your pain as the way that your body and brain is wired to respond to a breakup, rather than thinking it hurts so much because your ex was truly that special. I'm not trying to diminish the significance of your relationship but merely help you view your breakup pain in a different way that will allow you to take your power back.

HOW TO MOVE ON

Even though you may really like or love someone, it doesn't mean they're your best match, or that the relationship will work out. Relationships are like a living entity that requires so much more than the feeling of love to thrive. You need to be able to communicate effectively, speak each other's love languages, soothe each other's long-standing emotional injuries and attachment wounds, invest balanced effort, share a vision for the future that you're working toward together, and operate from a teammate mentality, with a "we factor" instead of a "me factor." When you've gone through a breakup, there's usually a piece of this larger puzzle that's missing. That said, a relationship ending doesn't mean it wasn't successful or didn't serve a purpose. Sometimes this experience is a stepping-stone to help you figure out what you really want and need. It's a love lesson. Love lessons are nuggets of wisdom you gain from thoughtfully reflecting on your relationship experiences so you can take away greater meaning and understanding. These ultimately help you move forward and find a better match.

Oftentimes you're not the same person at the end of the relationship as you were at the beginning. Part of your breakup struggle is figuring out who you are on your own and not in relation to your ex, and whether you have to return any borrowed parts or hold on to them as part of your new identity. As you strengthen your self-concept and continue to grow and evolve, keep perspective that this relationship and partner was simply a segment of your life, not your whole world. When you're struggling to move on, or lost in swirling negative thoughts about your breakup, meditate on the following affirmations:

When my heart breaks, it's opening for new love.

I existed before my ex, and I will exist after them.

I have survived all the difficult and painful moments of my past, which have made me stronger, wiser, and more resilient, and I will get through this, too.

When I stop searching for worthiness outside of myself and focus on creating it from within, I can welcome and embrace love into my life.

The bad and painful things in life put me on the path to the best things that will ever happen. Be patient and trust.

Some good things must come to an end so even better things can fall into place.

HOW TO BE OPENHEARTED ONCE AGAIN

Reopening your heart to love after you've been hurt is one of the most vulnerable things you can do. In order to feel love again, you have to accept the fact that you could also be hurt again. The good news is that you'll be reentering the dating market with clarity and a new direction. Though there's no guarantee you won't experience another heartbreak, feel confident that you're wiser this time around. Every time a relationship doesn't work out, you should be reflecting on your love lessons by asking yourself what you did and didn't like about yourself in this relationship, what you did and didn't like about your partner, how this relationship validated or challenged your internalized beliefs about how others will treat you, and what positive and negative traits and behaviors it brought out in you. Spend time thinking about the ways in which you did and did not feel loved by your ex, identify where the relationship was successful, as well as what was lacking. Ask yourself how you honored or ignored your needs in the partnership, and how you compromised too much. Get clear on what you absolutely must have in a future partnership in order to commit, and any different deal breakers that you will stand by the next time around. These love lessons will direct you toward a more ideal match and new love. You're so brave to believe in a bigger love— something more fulfilling, caring, and beautiful than you experienced in the past.

One mistake I often see people make when getting back out there after heartbreak is comparing every new potential partner to their ex. Stop looking for a Frankenboyfriend— someone who has all of the qualities you adored about your ex with the addition of what they were lacking. This mythical creature doesn't exist, and the more you search for another version of your ex, the more closed off you are to meeting someone new, who could have surprising qualities that make a better fit. Stop looking backward; you won't be able to see what's in front of you.

Having high standards for how you want to be treated is different from having unrealistic expectations. Are you asking too much of one person? Get your expectations in check. Expecting our partner to be our everything—our best friend, activity partner, business confidant, travel buddy, fitness coach, even the nurturing parent we never had—puts unfair pressure on the relationship. You're doomed to be disappointed because it's impossible for one person to fulfill all of these roles. When you start dating with a fulfilling life (go back to step 1!), you'll already have friends and family in these supportive roles, and you'll be able to open your heart from a place of *want* rather than *need*. When you're searching for a romantic partner, look for happiness, not perfection.

You'll know you're on the right track after heartbreak when you're able to see that this fresh start is exactly what you need to find a more ideal match. Now that you're an expert at practicing abundant thinking, this is the time to affirm that there are so many wonderful people out there with whom you can form a fulfilling, happy relationship. Life doesn't always go as planned, but sometimes unexpected experiences can lead us to an even better outcome. Trust that you will meet someone. Trust that timing has a way of working itself out. Trust that you are worthy and deserving of epic love.

KEY TAKEAWAYS

Breakups are inevitably part of the dating process, but unfortunately that doesn't make them any less painful. If you're still struggling with a soul-crushing breakup and need more support, read my book *Breaking Up & Bouncing Back: Moving on to Create the Love Life You Deserve*. Here are your step 7 takeaways:

- 💜 Without labeling them as good and bad, sit with your feelings and identify each one, which helps regulate your emotions and make them less intense.

- 💜 In the right relationship, your head and heart will align; you won't have to choose between them.

- 💜 Expect to go through the stages of breakup grief, which include denial, bargaining and anxiety, anger, depression, and eventually acceptance.

- 💜 Instead of acting out or seeking revenge, try healthy coping skills that naturally boost your mood and decrease symptoms of depression and anxiety.

- 💜 Figure out if you were more in love with the *idea* of your ex, and identify ways they weren't your best match, and how you weren't your best self in the relationship.

- 💜 Reframe your breakup pain as a physiological response to the withdrawal from love.

- 💜 Reflect on your love lessons so you can take away greater meaning and understanding of the relationship, and move forward to pick a better match.

- 💜 Reopening your heart to love requires vulnerability, that you look forward instead of backward, and realistic expectations of happiness, not perfection.

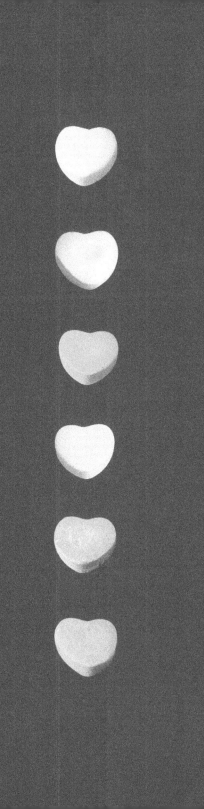

YOU GOT THIS

Congrats on finishing this book—you are now one big step closer to creating the love life you deserve! I hope you're able to focus less on your feelings of frustration about your past dating experiences and bring your attention toward cultivating enthusiasm, knowing and trusting you will meet your match. Your person is out there. How amazing is it that you will get to experience the joy of falling love? There is so much to look forward to.

In your dating journey, you're taking the time to meet yourself, letting go of old narratives and shame stories so that you can love yourself and honor your worth. You're not letting your stinkin' thinkin' and scarcity-driven fears get you down, and you are engaging in compassionate, abundant thoughts. You're crushing goals and filling your life with hobbies and passions that give you purpose. You're getting clear on your core values and the lifestyle you want, and choosing dating criteria based upon these factors, as well as shared goals and personality traits. You're also figuring out and setting firm deal breakers and being careful not to get overly consumed by sex appeal. You're now aware of your attachment style and how your attachment system gets triggered and influences your dating behaviors. You're striving to date from a secure mind-set. You're one woke woman and in your empowered energy you believe you have so much to offer a lucky partner.

You're practicing embracing your own imperfections, as well as a potential partner's, since there's no such thing as a perfect person. You're keeping an open mind, managing expectations, and taking advantage of all the places to meet someone—online, IRL, and through your friend and extended network. You're constantly putting yourself out there with a "hostess of the party" mentality and being conscious of your nonverbal behaviors and facial expressions so that you're approachable. Before dates, you're pumping yourself up with excitement, power poses, and getting in touch with your sexual, feminine energy. You're dressing in ways that reflect who you are on the inside, and you're projecting confidence instead of leading with insecurities.

On a date, you're present, engaging, authentic, and vulnerable, having deep conversations and learning about what matters most to the person across from you. You're being flirty and enjoying yourself. You're leaving them wanting more, and in the downtime between dates you're thoughtfully reflecting about *why* you want to see this person again. When you're dating secure, you're not rushing things or putting your life on hold, you set boundaries, and you know you're worthy of value and respect. As you begin to see someone more regularly, you peel back each other's layers, look for consistency, and eventually commit to each other to give the relationship the nurturing it needs so you can grow in love.

Now that you're equipped with an abundance of knowledge, skills, and strategies, I'm so excited for what's to come in your love life, and I hope you are, too. You got this, girl!

RESOURCES

Attached: The New Science of Adult Attachment and How It Can Help You Find—And Keep—Love by Amir Levine and Rachel Heller, 2012.

Breaking Up & Bouncing Back: Moving on to Create the Love Life You Deserve by Samantha Burns, 2018.

Why Him? Why Her?: How to Find and Keep Lasting Love by Helen Fisher, 2009.

REFERENCES

Alleyne, Richard. "Watch Out Lotharios: Faking Romantic Feelings Can Actually Lead to the Real Thing." *The Telegraph*. July 4, 2012. https://www.telegraph.co.uk/news/science/science-news/9373087/Watch-out-lotharios-Faking-romantic-feelings-can-actually-lead-to-the-real-thing.html.

AMAZE Org. "Consent Explained." YouTube. Dec 22, 2016. https://www.youtube.com/watch?v=5vmsfhw-czA.

Anwar, Yasmin. "Creating Love in the Lab: The 36 Questions That Spark Intimacy." *Berkeley News*. February 12, 2015. https://news.berkeley.edu/2015/02/12/love-in-the-lab/.

Aron, Arthur, Edward Melinat, Elaine N. Aron, Robert Darrin Vallone, and Renee J. Bator. "The Experimental Generation of Interpersonal Closeness: A Procedure and Some Preliminary Findings." *Personality and Social Psychology Bulletin* 23, no. 4 (April 1997): 363–377. doi:10.1177/0146167297234003.

Association for Psychological Science. "Grin and Bear It! Smiling Facilitates Stress Recovery." July 30, 2012. https://www.psychologicalscience.org/news/releases/smiling-facilitates-stress-recovery.html.

Bame, Yael. "53% of Millennial Women Have Received a Naked Photo from a Man." YouGov. October 9, 2017. https://today.yougov.com/topics/lifestyle/articles-reports/2017/10/09/53-millennial-women-have-received-dick-pic.

Boelens, Peter A., Roy R. Reeves, William H. Replogle, and Harold G. Koenig. "A Randomized Trial of the Effect of Prayer on Depression and Anxiety." *The International Journal of Psychiatry in Medicine* 39, no. 4 (December 2009): 377–92. doi:10.2190/PM.39.4.c.

Brooks, Alison. "Get Excited: Reappraising Pre-Performance Anxiety as Excitement." *Journal of Experimental Psychology: General* 143, no. 3 (June 2014): 1144–1158. doi:10.1037/a0035325.

Brown, Brené. *Daring Greatly: How the Courage to Be Vulnerable Transforms the Way We Live, Love, Parent, and Lead.* New York: Avery Publishing, 2015.

Brown, Brené. *The Gifts of Imperfection: Let Go of Who You Think You're Supposed to Be and Embrace Who You Are.* Center City, Minnesota: Hazeldon Publishing, 2010.

Burns, Samantha. *Breaking up & Bouncing Back: Moving On to Create the Love Life You Deserve.* Mineola, New York: Ixia Press, 2018.

Buytshirtsonline. "The Perception of Colour." http://www .buytshirtsonline.co.uk/colour-perception.

Chapman, Gary. *The Five Love Languages: How to Express Heartfelt Commitment to Your Mate.* Sydney: Strand Publishing, 2000.

Cuddy, Amy J. C., S. Jack Schultz, and Nathan E. Fosse. "P-Curving a More Comprehensive Body of Research on Postural Feedback Reveals Clear Evidential Value for Power-Posing Effects: Reply to Simmons and Simonsohn (2017)." *Psychological Science* 29, no. 4 (April 2018): 656–66. doi:10.1177/0956797617746749.

Elliot, Andrew J. and Daniela Niesta. "Romantic Red: Red Enhances Men's Attraction to Women." *Journal of Personality and Social Psychology* 95, no. 5 (2008): 1150 –1164. doi:10.1037/0022-3514.95.5.1150.

Fisher, Helen E. *Anatomy of Love: A Natural History of Mating, Marriage, and Why We Stray.* New York: W.W. Norton & Company, 2017.

Goldstein, Pavel, Irit Weissman-Fogel, and Simone G. Shamay-Tsoory. "The Role of Touch in Regulating Inter-Partner Physiological Coupling During Empathy for Pain." *Scientific Reports* 7, no. 1 (June 12, 2017): 3252. doi:10.1038/s41598-017-03627-7.

Gutman, Sharon A., and Victoria P. Schindler. "The Neurological Basis of Occupation." *Occupational Therapy International* 14, no. 2 (2007): 71–85. doi:10.1002/oti.225.

Headlee, Celeste, "10 Ways to Have a Better Conversation." TEDxCreativeCoast. May 2015. https://www.ted.com/talks/celeste_headlee_10_ways_to_have_a_better_conversation#t-375345.

Hughes, Susan M., Marissa A. Harrison, and Gordon G. Gallup, Jr. "Sex Differences in Romantic Kissing among College Students: An Evolutionary Perspective." *Evolutionary Psychology* 5, no. 3 (July 2007). doi:10.1177/147470490700500310.

Jones, Daniel. "The 36 Questions That Lead to Love." *The New York Times*. January 9, 2015. https://www.nytimes.com/2015/01/11/fashion/no-37-big-wedding-or-small.html.

Khoshkam, Samira, Fatemeh Bahrami, S. Ahmad Ahmadi, Maryam Fatehizade, and Ozra Etemadi. "Attachment Style and Rejection Sensitivity: The Mediating Effect of Self-Esteem and Worry Among Iranian College Students." *Europe's Journal of Psychology* 8, no. 3 (2012): 363–374. doi:10.5964/ejop.v8i3.463.

Kross, Ethan, Marc G. Berman, Walter Mischel, Edward E. Smith, and Tor D. Wager. "Social Rejection Shares Somatosensory Representations with Physical Pain." *Proceedings of the National Academy of Sciences* 108, no. 15 (April 2011): 6270–6275. doi:10.1073/pnas.1102693108.

Levine, Amir, and Rachel Heller. *Attached: The New Science of Adult Attachment and How It Can Help You Find—and Keep—Love.* New York, NY: TarcherPerigee, 2012.

Lewis, Thomas, Fari Amini, and Richard Lannon. *A General Theory of Love.* New York: Vintage Books, 2001.

Lieberman, Matthew D., Tristen K. Inagaki, Golnaz Tabibnia, and Molly J. Crockett. "Subjective Responses to Emotional Stimuli During Labeling, Reappraisal, and Distraction." *Emotion* 11, no. 3 (2011): 468–80. doi:10.1037/a0023503.

Lindig, Sarah. "This Is the Best Color to Wear on a First Date." *Harper's Bazaar.* August 29, 2015. https://www.harpersbazaar .com/fashion/trends/a11982/best-color-to-wear-for-every -occasion/.

Lindquist, Kristen. "Does Labeling Your Feelings Help Regulate Them?" *Emotion News.* September 9, 2016. http://emotionnews .org/does-labeling-your-feelings-help-regulate-them/.

Lisitsa, Ellie. "The Four Horsemen: Criticism, Contempt, Defensive-ness, and Stonewalling." The Gottman Institute. April 23, 2013. https://www.gottman.com/blog/the-four-horsemen-recognizing -criticism-contempt-defensiveness-and-stonewalling/.

Match. "Match Releases New Study on LGBTQ Single Population." May 24, 2016. http://match.mediaroom.com/2016-05-24 -Match-Releases-New-Study-On-LGBTQ-Single-Population.

Match. "Singles in America (2015 Survey)." http://www.singlesin america.com/2016.

Match. "Singles in America (2017 Survey)." http://www.singlesin america.com/2018.

McCorquodale, Amanda. "8 'Fake It 'Til You Make It' Strategies Backed by Science." *Mental Floss.* February 2, 2016. http://mentalfloss.com/article/74310/8-fake-it-til-you-make-it -strategies-backed-science.

Mehl, Matthias R., Simine Vazire, Shannon E. Holleran, and C. Shelby Clark. "Eavesdropping on Happiness: Well-Being Is Related to Having Less Small Talk and More Substantive Conversations." *Psychological Science* 21, no. 4 (April 2010): 539–41. doi:10.1177/0956797610362675.

Reddit. "What's your favorite response to unsolicited dick pics?" r/AskWomen. 2018. https://www.reddit.com/r/AskWomen /comments/985ww0/whats_your_favorite_response_to _unsolicited_dick/.

Riley, Jill, Betsan Corkhill, and Clare Morris. "The Benefits of Knitting for Personal and Social Wellbeing in Adulthood: Findings from an International Survey." *British Journal of Occupational Therapy* 76, no. 2 (February 2013): 50–57. doi:10.4276 /030802213X13603244419077.

Saxbe, Darby, and Rena L. Repetti. "For Better or Worse? Coregulation of Couples' Cortisol Levels and Mood States." *Journal of Personality and Social Psychology* 98, no. 1 (2010): 92–103. doi: 10.1037/a0016959.

Shrira, Ilan. "'Fake It Till You Make It' Turns Out to Be a Good Strategy." *Psychology Today.* January 2, 2016. https://www .psychologytoday.com/us/blog/the-narcissus-in-all-us/201601 /fake-it-till-you-make-it-turns-out-be-good-strategy.

Smith, Jeremy Adam. "The Subversive Power of the Kiss." *Greater Good.* February 11, 2016. https://greatergood.berkeley.edu /article/item/subversive_power_of_the_kiss.

Staufenberg, Jess. "Being Friends in a Relationship Is 'Most Important Factor' for Sex Life and Longevity." *The Independent.* May 4, 2016. https://www.independent.co.uk/life-style /love-sex/being-friends-in-a-relationship-is-most-important -factor-for-sex-life-and-longevity-a7012616.html.

Tatkin, Stan. *Wired for Dating: How Understanding Neurobiology and Attachment Style Can Help You Find Your Ideal Mate.* Oakland, CA: New Harbinger Publications, 2016.

VanderDrift, Laura E., Juan E. Wilson, and Christopher R. Agnew. "On the Benefits of Valuing Being Friends for Nonmarital Romantic Partners." *Journal of Social and Personal Relationships* 30, no. 1 (February 2013): 115–31. doi:10.1177 /0265407512453009.

Verderosa, Andy. "Any App Is a Dating App if You Try Hard Enough." *Thrillist.* February 18, 2016. https://www.thrillist .com/sex-dating/nation/how-to-use-regular-apps-as-dating -apps?fbclid=IwAR0CpLGO7r039ZvABjlJH50Zu7mqy4Pk -U8HWA03vdMCMZz3KLNfjUSiDFk.

Whitbourne, Susan Krauss. "7 Ways to Make Small Talk Work for You." *Psychology Today.* September 6, 2014. https://www .psychologytoday.com/us/blog/fulfillment-any-age/201409 /7-ways-make-small-talk-work-you.

Wlodarski, Rafael, and Robin I. M. Dunbar. "Examining the Possible Functions of Kissing in Romantic Relationships." *Archives of Sexual Behavior* 42, no. 8 (2013): 1415–23. doi:10.1007/ s10508-013-0190-1.

"What's in a Kiss? The Effect of Romantic Kissing on Mating Desirability." *Evolutionary Psychology: An International Journal of Evolutionary Approaches to Psychology and Behavior* 12, no. 1 (March 19, 2014): 178–99. https://www.ncbi.nlm.nih.gov/pmc/articles/PMC4487818/.

Wolpert, Stuart. "Putting Feelings into Words Produces Therapeutic Effects in the Brain; UCLA Neuroimaging Study Supports Ancient Buddhist Teachings." UCLA Newsroom. June 21, 2007. http://newsroom.ucla.edu/releases/Putting-Feelings-Into-Words-Produces-8047.

Yim, JongEun. "Therapeutic Benefits of Laughter in Mental Health: A Theoretical Review." *The Tohoku Journal of Experimental Medicine* 239, no. 3 (2016): 243–249. doi:10.1620/tjem.239.243.

ACKNOWLEDGMENTS

The decision to write this book was made on the day that I gave birth to my daughter, Talia Rose. I happened to be lying on a hospital bed waiting to dilate (seriously!), hours away from Talia making her grand entrance, when an opportunity presented itself to bring my dating advice to the masses. I'm so passionate about helping women become more confident, empowered daters that despite the chaotic timing of becoming a first-time mom, I knew this book also deserved to be birthed into the world. A dating-centric book fit perfectly as the next piece to follow my first book, *Breaking Up & Bouncing Back*. So as I got my new mom legs beneath me, I also committed to writing and sharing my knowledge and client work with all of you. Just as it takes a village to raise a child, you also can't write and publish a book all on your own. A heartfelt thank you to my editor, Pippa White, and the staff at Callisto Media for bringing this inspirational and supportive book to life. Deep gratitude for my parents and friends who cheered me on and made me feel like Superwoman as a new mom while I hunkered down to write. Most important, thank you to my husband for being the type of partner I knew deep down that I deserved, but hadn't yet allowed myself to fall for until I practiced falling in love with myself. Thank you for putting up with my shenanigans in our early dating days, for helping me to heal and trust, and for modeling a secure attachment style. We have created a magical life. I can't wait to raise our daughter to be confident, vulnerable, and strong and to show her what healthy love looks like. My wish for Talia is that she has the self-worth to realize she deserves a partner who treats her as well as you treat me.

ABOUT THE AUTHOR

 **SAMANTHA BURNS** MA, LMHC, the Millennial Love Expert, is a licensed counselor, dating coach, and author of *Breaking Up & Bouncing Back: Moving on to Create the Love Life You Deserve.* She runs a private practice in Boston, coaches clients across the country through breakups, dating, and relationships, and is the founder of the transformational *Breakup Bounce Back* coaching program. She's been recognized by Match as one of the leading love experts in the industry, is often consulted by Tinder to decode dating behavior, and featured in the media, including *Women's Health, Cosmopolitan, HuffPost, Refinery29, Bustle, Elite Daily, Reader's Digest, Business Insider, USA Today,* the *Boston Globe,* and many more. To learn more about her and her services, visit www.lovesuccessfully.com.

CPSIA information can be obtained
at www.ICGtesting.com
Printed in the USA
LVHW051839231219
641485LV00019B/1735/P